BRECON TO NEWPORT

Vic Mitchell and Keith Smith
in association with Dave Edge

MP Middleton Press

Cover picture: Also in the last photograph in this book, 0-6-0 no. 2247 enhances the scene at Brecon on 17th September 1962, as it blows off prior to departure for Newport. (R.E.Toop)

First Published November 2003

ISBN 1 904474 16 0

© Middleton Press, 2003

Design   Deborah Esher
            David Pede
Typesetting   Barbara Mitchell

Published by
            Middleton Press
            Easebourne Lane
            Midhurst, West Sussex
            GU29 9AZ
Tel: 01730 813169
Fax: 01730 812601
Email: info@middletonpress.co.uk
www.middletonpress.co.uk

Printed & bound by MPG Books, Bodmin, Cornwall

INDEX

I. Route map in the 1950s. (Atlantic Publishers)

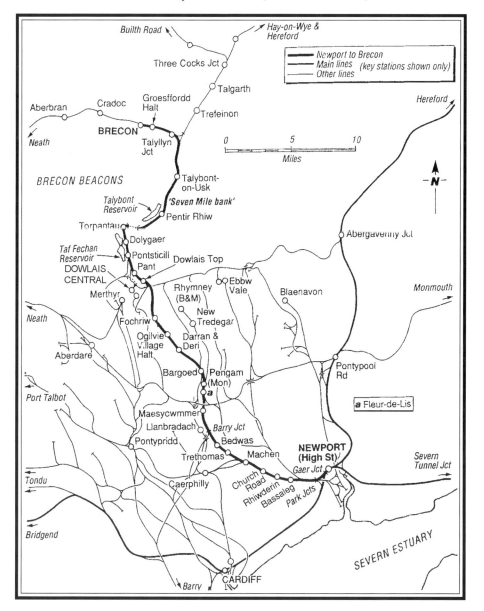

ACKNOWLEDGEMENTS

We are very grateful for the assistance received from many of those mentioned in the credits also from W.R.Burton, R.Caston (Welsh Railways Research Circle), L.Crosier, G.Croughton, D.Dobbins, J.Gardener, G.Heathcliffe, E.Hancock, A.J.Hills, F.Hornby, M.Johns, N.Langridge, H.Morgan, Mr D. and Dr S.Salter, N.Seabourne, G.T.V.Stacey, M.J.Stretton, M.Turvey, H.Williams and especially our wives, Barbara Mitchell and Janet Smith.

GEOGRAPHICAL SETTING

For long termed Brecknockshire, the county's principal town was Brecon, which accommodated an army garrison and a small cathedral. Situated at the confluence of the River Usk and the Honddu, it was an important market town and administrative centre.

The route did not take the easy course down the Usk Valley, but climbed steeply (partly in tunnel) to Talyllyn Junction before descending to cross the Usk north of Talybont. Here began a gruelling climb of almost seven miles at 1 in 38 up the valley of the Caerfanell and alongside Talybont Reservoir to ascend the north face of the mighty Brecon Beacons. The area is largely composed of Old Red Sandstone.

A watershed was reached at the summit at Torpantau Tunnel and an amazing height of 1313ft above sea level was attained. The journey to Talybont was largely through fertile agricultural land, but south thereof it was in partially wooded mountainous terrain, very thinly populated, as far as Pant. Thereafter, the landscape changed dramatically and the views included numerous industrial scars.

Ironmaking had begun in about 1760 and four massive furnaces were polluting the environment in about 20 years. Within the next 40, there were over 150 miles of tramroads in the area supplying them with coal from the numerous small pits. From Limestone outcrops in these remote uplands, other tramroads were conveying it to the giant works where it was used as a flux in iron and eventually steel making.

The urbanised area of Dowlais developed at a great altitude and thus looked down upon Merthyr, the coal measures being south of these places. The route was in a dip in this area before climbing to its second summit of 1314ft, about two miles south of Dowlais Top.

A steep descent followed to the Rhymney Valley at Bargoed, the gradient easing until the line turned eastward on its approach to Bedwas. A more level course followed to Machen, where the Rhymney River turns south, but the track continues eastwards on its steady descent to Newport. Limestone from a quarry at Machen continues to

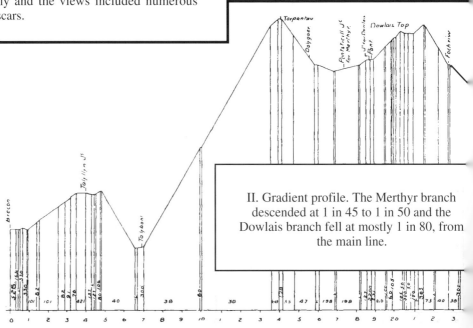

II. Gradient profile. The Merthyr branch descended at 1 in 45 to 1 in 50 and the Dowlais branch fell at mostly 1 in 80, from the main line.

provide traffic for this section of the line.

The southern part of the route was close to the border of Glamorganshire and Monmouthshire and ended in the latter at Newport which developed its extensive docks at the mouth of the River Usk. The town is on the headland at the confluence of the Usk and the Ebbw River, and, after a period in Gwent, it is now in Monmouthshire again. However, this is now part of Wales.

The maps are to the scale of 25ins to 1 mile with north at the top, unless otherwise indicated.

HISTORICAL BACKGROUND

Most of the area south of the Brecon Beacons was heavily industrialised and thus had a very extensive system of horse-worked tramroads long before the arrival of the main line railway.

The first such route was the South Wales Railway's line between Chepstow and Swansea, which opened on 18th June 1850. It became part of the Great Western Railway in 1862 and its broad gauge tracks were converted to standard in 1872.

The Brecon & Merthyr Tydfil Junction Railway (the B&M or BMR) obtained an Act on 1st August 1859 to construct a line between Talybont and Pant. It was intended that the section between Brecon and Talybont would be built on the route of the 1816 Hay Tramroad, but the Hay, Hereford & Brecon Railway planned to take most of it. The BMR secured the section west of Talyllyn however, but had to enlarge the tunnel and allow other trains to use it, together with the line into Brecon. Train service between Brecon and Pant began on 23rd April 1863, but the company was receivership from 1866 until 1870.

Talyllyn became a junction on 19th September 1864, when the HHBR opened; trains to Hereford were the responsibility of the BMR until the Midland Railway took over in 1869.

The next BMR section to open was from Pontsticill to Cefn, on the Merthyr branch, on 1st August 1867. Trains ran over other companies' tracks to Merthyr High Street from 1st August 1868. Pant to Dowlais (Central from 1924) was opened on 23rd June 1869 by the BMR.

The BMR route from Pant to Dowlais Top opened on 1st August 1867 and the service was extended to Pengam on 1st August 1868, partly over foreign tracks. Darran-Bargoed was Rhymney Railway property, while the line south of Bassaleg was later owned by the Great Western Railway. Between these two sections, the BMR had acquired and relaid the 1825 Rumney Tramroad. Service began between Pengam and Newport (Dock Street) on 14th June 1865. The BMR's branch from Pengam to Rhymney opened on 16th April 1866, but is not included in this volume; neither is the Machen-Caerphilly section, which came into use on 7th July 1884.

The BMR comprised 82 route miles when it was absorbed into the GWR, along with some of its neighbours, on 1st July 1922. The lines became part of the Western Region of British Railways upon nationalisation in 1948.

The Dowlais Central branch lost its regular passenger service on 28th June 1952, but trains for workmen continued until 2nd May 1960. The Brecon-Newport route closed to passengers in its entirety on 31st December 1962; the goods closures are given in the captions. An exception was the Machen-Newport section which had a workmen's service to and from Caerphilly until 1st July 1963.

Freight trains ran to Trethomas until 1987 and continued to operate to Machen Quarry in 2003.

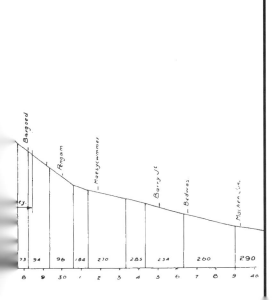

PASSENGER SERVICES

We always consider in this section trains running in the down direction. However, in the valleys of South Wales this means downhill and not down from London.

The initial service between Brecon and Pant offered two trains, weekdays only, and that between Pengam and Newport in 1865 comprised three on weekdays and two on Sundays. There were very few trains on Sundays on any part of the route subsequently.

Most accounts of the route state that there were usually four through trains. However, there were only three until 1902, the figure of four applying to most subsequent years. From Pengam southwards, there were an extra three or four trains from the Rhymney Valley to supplement the service to Newport. Termination of trains here was at Dock Street until 1880 and at High Street thereafter.

There were some other short workings, notably for the benefit of workmen. There were also some extras for holidaymakers, such as Merthyr-Aberystwyth and Barry-Llandrindod Wells. These ran from about 1890 to 1914, with a few restored briefly after World War I. They ran via the east curve at Talyllyn Junction, not calling at the station. A few of these trains from Central Wales ran to the terminus at either Merthyr or Dowlais.

Dowlais Central Branch

Provided weekdays only, the service frequency in selected years is shown below:

1870	6	1939	8
1895	6	1951	8
1923	7		

There were some additional trips for workmen and initially there were a few trains on Sundays. Most of these reversed at Pant and served stations to the south.

BRECON, MERTHYR, DOWLAIS, RHYMNEY, and NEWPORT.—Brecon and Merthyr.
Traff. Man., J. Gall, Newport (Mon.) Sec., H. R. Price, 132, Palmerston Buildings, E.C.

Fares. 1 cl.	2 cl.	3 cl.	New Joint Station	mrn	mrn	mrn	aft	aft	aft	aft	aft
			Brecon ......dep.	....	7 50	....	....	2 5	5 5	....	
0 9	0 6	0 4	Talyllyn Junction	....	8 4	....	....	2 25	5 20	....	
1 3	0 10	0 7	Talybont	....	8 12	....	....	2 32	5 28	....	
2 6	1 9	1 2	Torpantau........	....	Sig.	....	....	Sig.	Sig.	....	
3 0	2 0	1 8½	Dolygaer	....	8 36	....	....	2 58	5 52	....	
3 4	2 4	1 5½	Pontsticill Junc.	....	8 40	....	....	3 2	5 57	....	Saturdays only.
....	....	....	Pontsticill Junc.	....	8 53	10 5		3 10	6 6	7 55	
3 9	2 10	1 7½	Pontsarn *.......	....	....	Sig.		Sig.	Sig.	Sig.	
4 0	3 0	1 9½	Cefn ....[46, 48	....	9 5	1017		3 20	6 18	8 10	
4 3	3 3	2 0	Merthyr 61, arr.	....	9 15	1027		3 30	6 28	8 20	
3 11	2 9	1 7	Pant Junction....	....	8 47	Stop	Saturdays only.	3 19	6 5	Stop	
4 2	2 11	1 8	Dowlais 304, 305 arr.	....	9 0			3 30	6 20		
			Dowlais 304, 305 dep.	....	8 35	....		2 37	5 50	....	
4 3	3 0	1 8½	Dowlais Top......	....	8 53	....		3 28	6 12	....	
4 10	3 5	1 11½	Fochriw	....	9 0	....		3 36	6 22	....	
5 0	3 6	2 2	Darran......[305	....	9 6	....		3 44	6 32	....	
5 0	3 6	2 4½	Bargoed Junc. 304,	....	9 11	aft		3 52	6 40	aft	
5 0	3 6	2 10½	Rhymney ..dep.	8 5	....	1 10		3 10	....	6 0	7 55
5 0	3 6	2 8	New Tredegar †.	8 11	....	1 18		3 20	....	6 8	8 2
....	....	....	Aberbargoed ...	Sig.	....	Sig.		Sig.	....	Sig.	Sig.
....	....	....	Pengam ....arr.	8 20	....	1 27		3 30	....	6 18	8 11
5 0	3 6	2 6	Pengam	8 21	9 17	1 28		4 1	6 49	6 19	8 12
5 3	3 9	2 8	Maesycwmmer	8 27	9 22	1 34	1 34	4 6	6 56	6 25	8 18
6 0	4 0	3 0½	Bedwas	8 37	9 32	....	1 43	4 15	7 5	....	8 28
7 0	4 6	3 3½	Machen 62	8 45	9 40	....	1 50	4 23	7 14	....	8 35
7 0	4 6	3 5	Church Road......	8 51	9 45	....	1 56	4 27	7 20	....	8 41
7 6	5 0	3 7	Rhiwderin	8 57	9 50	....	2 2	4 31	7 26	....	8 46
7 6	5 0	3 8	Bassaleg 53 [48, 59	9 5	10 0	....	2 10	4 36	7 36	....	8 52
8 0	5 0	3 11	Newport 51 to 55.	9 15	1010	....	2 20	4 45	7 45	....	9 0

	mrn	mrn	aft	aft	aft	aft	aft
Newport......dep.	8 25	1110	1 40	4 35	....	5 50	9 30
Bassaleg	8 34	1120	1 49	4 44	....	6 0	9 38
Rhiwderin........	8 38	1125	1 53	4 48	....	6 7	9 43
Church Road......	8 43	1130	1 58	4 53	....	6 13	9 49
Machen	8 48	1135	2 3	4 59	....	6 20	9 56
Bedwas	8 55	1142	2 10	5 6	....	6 28	10 3
Maesycwmmer	9 4	1152	2 19	5 15	6 31	6 35	1012
Pengam	9 9	1157	2 23	5 20	6 35	6 44	1017
Pengam ....dep.	....	12 5	2 28	5 21	5 50		1018
Aberbargoed	....	Sig.	Sig.	Sig.	Sig.	....	Sig.
New Tredegar †.	....	1212	2 35	5 30	7 0	....	1028
Rhymney 304 a	....	1220	2 45	5 40	7 10	....	1035
Bargoed Junc. 304	9 22	Stop	2 29	Saturdays only.	Stop	6 55	Saturdays only.
Darran ......[305	9 29		2 34			7 2	
Fochriw	9 38	....	2 41		....	7 12	
Dowlais Top......	9 46	....	2 49		....	7 22	
Dowlais 304, 305 arr.	10 5	aft	3 30		....	7 40	
Dowlais 304, 305 dep.	9 35	12 5	2 37		....	7 15	
Pant Junction....	9 52	1210	2 55		aft	7 28	
Merthyr ...dep	9 38	1210	2 37		5 30	7 15	
Cefn............	9 47	1220	2 45		5 40	7 25	
Pontsarn *.......	Sig.	Sig.	Sig.		Sig.	Sig.	
Pontsticill Jn. a	9 57	1233	2 55		5 52	7 35	
Pontsticill Junc...	10 0	1236	3 2		....	7 40	
Dolygaer	10 5	1241	3 7		....	7 45	
Torpantau........	Sig.	Sig.	Sig.		....	Sig.	
Talybont ....[308	1032	1 5	3 30		....	8 10	
Talyllyn Jn. 405,	1040	1 12	3 38		....	8 18	
Brecon 405 ..arr.	1055	1 35	3 50		....	8 30	

* Station for Vaynor. † New Tredegar and Whiterose.

December 1

BRECON, RHYMNEY, and NEWPORT.—Great Western (late Brecon and Merthyr).

Week Days only.

Miles	Down.	mrn	mrn	mrn	mrn	mrn	mrn	non	aft	aft	aft	aft	aft	aft	aft	aft	aft	aft	aft	aft	aft	aft	aft
—	Brecon ....dep.			7 35				12 0				2 5	2 45					6 8					Saturdays only.
4¼	Talyllyn Junction arr.			7 45				1210				2 15	2 55					6 18					
	Talyllyn Junction dep.			7 47				1215				2 30	3 0					6 23					
7	Talybont-on-Usk			7 57				1225				2 40	3 10					6 33					
—	Pentir Rhiw			8 9				1236				2s50	3 22					6u45					
14¼	Torpantau			8 20				1249				3 3	3 23					6 56					
15¾	Dolygaer			8 24				1253				3 7	3 37					7 0					
17¾	Pontsticill Junction 86. arr.			8 29				1258				3 12	3 41					7 5			6 20		
24½	Merthyr 86 arr			9 16				1 40				3 40	4 2					7 40			6 46		
	Merthyr 86 dep.			8 10		8 45		1210	1225	2 10	1249	2 45		4 15			5 30				6 55	9 35	
—	Pontsticill Junction ....dep.			8 36			8β40	1 6			1 14	3 24	3 45					7 10					
19	Pant 86 ....arr.			8 39			8β44	1 9			1 18	3 27	3 49					7 13					
20½	Dowlais § 86 arr.			8 50			8β50				1 24	3F45	3 55					7 25					
	Dowlais § 86 dep.			8 25			Stop				Stop	3 20			4s40	5s25		6 55					915
—	Pant ....dep.			8 42		Through Train, Merthyr to Newport, via Caerphilly, see page 93 and below.		1 12	Through Train, Merthyr to Newport, via Caerphilly, see page 93 and below.	Through Train, Merthyr to Newport, via Caerphilly, see page 93 and below.		3 28	Fridays only.	Through Train, Merthyr to Newport, via Caerphilly, see page 93 and below.	4s53	5s35	Through Train, Merthyr to Newport, via Caerphilly, see page 93 and below.	7 16			Through Train, Llandrindod Wells, to Barry, via Builth Wells, see pages 386, 142, 98, and 89.	Through Train, Merthyr to Newport, via Caerphilly, see page 93 and below.	927
20¼	Dowlais Top ‡			8 48				1 19				3 34			4s59	5s41		7 22					933
23¾	Fochriw			8 56				1 28				3 42			5s7	5 49		7 30		855			941
26½	Darran and Deri ....[82			9 3				1 36				3 49			5s14	5 56		7 37		9 1			948
28¼	Bargoed & Aber Bargoed ††			9 10				1 45				3 57			5s22	6 2		7 45		9 7			954
30	Pengam † 86 ....arr.			9 13			mrn	1 49			aft	4 2			5s27			7 51					
—	Mls Rhymney & Pontlottyn dep.	734	829		10 5		11 5	1s25			2 45				5 13				640				
—	1 Abertysswg	738	833		10 9		11 9	1s29			2 49				5 17				644				
—	2½ New Tredegar **	743	838		1014		1114	1s34			2 54				5 22				649				
—	3¾ Cwmsyfiog and Brithdir	747	842		1018		1118	1s38			2 58				5 26				653				
—	4¾ Bargoed & Aber Bargoed*	752	847		1022		1122	1s42			3 3				5 31				657				
—	5 Pengam † 86 ....arr.	757	852		1027		1127	1s46			3 8				5 36				7 2				
—	Pengam & Fleur-de-lis ..dep.	8 0	857	9 15	1030		1130	1 50			3 12	4 4			5 39			7 52	7 3				
31½	Maesycwmmer ¶	8 6	9 2	9 21	1036		1136	1 56			3 19	4 10			5 45			7 58	7 6				
36¼	Bedwas	817		9 32	1047		1148	2 7			3 30	4 21			5 56			8 9					
—	Trethomas	821		9 36	1051		1152	2 11			3 34	4 25			6 0			8s13					
39½	Machen 87....	829		9 44	1059		12 0	2 19			3 42	4 33			6 9			8 21					
40¾	Church Road	834		9 49	11 4		12 5	2 24			3 47	4 38			6 14			8 26					
43	Rhiwderin	840		9 55	1110		1211	2 30			3 53	4 44			6 20			8 32					
44	Bassaleg (B.M.) ‖ ....[123	845		10 0	1115		1215	2 35			3 57	4 48			6 25			8 35					
47	Newport ‡‡ 62, 67, 80, arr.	855		1010	1125	9 53	1226	2 45	1 30	3 20	4 8	4 59		5 22	6 35		6 40	8 47				1043	

b Fridays and Saturdays. β Tuesdays and Fridays, except on 30th instant. F Arrives at 3 55 aft on Fridays.
s Saturdays only. *u* Except Wednesdays and Thursdays.
† Pengam and Fleur-de-lis. ** New Tredegar and Tirphil. ‡‡ High Street.

October 192

BRECON, MERTHYR, DOWLAIS, RHYMNEY, and NEWPORT.—Brecon and Merthyr.

Traff. Man., J. Gall, Newport (Mon.)   Sec., H. R. Price, 132, Palmerston Buildings, E.C.

New Joint Station,	mrn	mrn	mrn	mrn	mrn	aft	aft	aft	aft	aft	aft	aft
					Mondays only.—In connection with Cambrian Train.	Thursdays only.						Saturdays only.
Brecon........dep.	....	7 45	....	....	....	8 10	1250	2 5	...	5 10	....	
Talyllyn Junction..	....	8 0	....	....	....	8 21	1 10	2 30	...	5 30	....	
Talybont-on-Usk....	....	8 8	....	....	1032	8 30	1 34	2 40	...	5 38	....	
Torpantau..........	....	Sig.	....	....	....	8 50	....	Sig.	...	Sig.	....	
Dolygaer...........	....	8 32	....	....	....	8 55	....	3 8	...	6 2	....	
Pontsticill Junction	....	8 36	....	....	....	9 0	2 5	3 12	...	6 6	....	
Pontsticill Jn.dep.	....	8 49	10 5	....	11 0	9 7	2 20	3 26	...	6 10	7 55	
Pontsarn *.........	....	Sig.	Sig.	....	....	9 15	Sig.	Sig.	...	Sig.	8 0	
Cefn ....[62	....	8 57	1019	....	1110	9 20	2 31	3 36	...	6 20	8 10	
Merthyr 80, 60, ar	....	9 7	1028	....	1120	9 30	2 40	3 45	...	6 29	8 20	
Pant Junction......	....	8 45	....	....		9 14	2 15	3 27	...	6 12	....	
395 Dowlais .. arr.	....	9 0	....	....		9 20	2 25	3 35	...	6 20	....	
395 Dowlais .. dep.	....	8 35	....	....			2 0	3 10	...	5 55	....	
Dowlais Top........	....	8 52	....	....			2 23	3 33	...	6 19	....	
Fochriw............	....	8 59	....	....			2 30	3 40	...	6 26	....	
Darran ....[395	....	9 5	....	....			2 35	3 48	...	6 32	....	
Bargoed Junc. 394,	....	9 15	....	....			2 43	3 57	...	6 40	....	
Rhymney ....dep.	7 50	....	....	1140			....	3 15	6 0	....	....	7 50
New Tredegar †...	7 57	....	....	1147			....	3 22	6 8	....	....	7 57
Aberbargoed......	8 2	....	....	1153			....	3 28	613	....	....	8 2
Pengam.......arr.	8 6	....	....	1157			....	3 33	618	....	....	8 6
Pengam............	8 7	9 20	....	1158			2 50	4 5	619	6 49	....	8 7
Maesycwmmer.......	8 12	9 24	....	12 3			2 55	4 10	625	6 55	....	8 11
Bedwas............	8 22	9 33	....	1212			3 5	4 19	...	7 4	....	8 20
Machen 76.........	8 29	9 39	....	1219			3 12	4 27	...	7 11	....	8 27
Church Road.......	8 34	9 43	....	1224			3 17	4 32	...	7 16	....	8 31
Rhiwderin.........	8 39	9 47	....	1230			3 23	4 37	...	7 21	....	8 35
Bassaleg 76.......	8 46	9 56	....	1240			3 35	4 45	...	7 35	....	8 41
Newport 64 to 73ar	8 55	10 5	....	1250			3 45	4 55	...	7 45	....	8 50

	mrn	mrn	mrn	aft	aft	aft	aft	aft	aft
			Through Carriages for Aberystwyth & Cambrian Line.						Saturdays only.
Newport........dep.	8 25	1010	1055	....	1 35	2 5	....	6 15	9 35
Bassaleg..........	8 34	1019	....	....	1 44	2 14	....	6 25	9 43
Rhiwderin.........	8 38	1023	....	....	1 48	2 18	....	6 29	9 48
Church Road.......	8 43	1028	....	....	1 53	2 23	....	6 34	9 54
Machen............	8 48	1033	....	....	1 58	2 28	....	6 39	10 0
Bedwas............	8 55	1040	....	....	2 5	2 35	....	6 46	10 8
Maesycwmmer.......	9 4	1049	b	....	2 14	2 44	....	6 55	1017
Pengam............	9 9	1054	1134	....	2 19	2 48	....	6 59	1021
Pengam.......dep.	....	1058	....	....	2 23	....	....	7 5	1022
Aberbargoed.......	....	11 2	....	....	2 27	....	....	7 10	1027
New Tredegar †....	a	11 8	....	....	2 35	....	....	7 18	1038
Rhymney 394 arr.	a	1115	....	....	2 42	....	....	7 25	1045
Bargoed Junc. 394,	9 22	....	1150	....	....	2 54	....	7 5	
Darran ....[395	9 29	....	1156	....	....	2 59	....	7 10	
Fochriw...........	9 38	....	12 4	....	....	3 7	....	7 18	
Dowlais Top.......	9 46	....	b	....	....	3 14	....	7 25	
395 Dowlais .. arr.	10 5	....	....	....	....	3 35	....	7 40	
395 Dowlais .. dep.	9 35	....	....	12 5	....	3 10	....	7 15	
Pant Junction.....	9 52	....	12 5	1210	....	3 19	....	7 30	
Merthyr......dep.	9 38	....	12 0	1210	....	2 50	5 30	7 15	
Cefn..............	9 47	....	1210	1220	....	3 0	5 40	7 25	
Pontsarn *........	Sig.	....	....	Sig.	....	Sig.	Sig.	Sig.	
Pontsticill Jn. arr.	9 57	....	1220	1231	....	3 10	5 52	7 35	
Pontsticill Junction	10 0	....	1230	1240	....	3 26	....	7 40	
Dolygaer..........	10 5	....	....	1245	....	3 30	....	7 45	
Torpantau.........	Sig.	....	....	Sig.	....	Sig.	....	Sig.	
Talybont-on-Usk...	1032	....	....	1 10	....	3 55	....	8 10	
Talyllyn J. 534, 400	1040	....	....	1 18	....	4 3	....	8 18	
Brecon 534.....arr.	11 0	....	....	1 40	....	4 15	....	8 30	

a Passengers for these Stations change at Bargoed, and proceed by Rhymney Train. b Stops to take up for the Cambrian Line on notice being given at the Station. * Station for Vaynor. † New Tredegar and Whiterose.

July 1903

Week Days only.

Down.	mn	mn	mn	mn	mn	mn	mrn	aft	aft	aft	aft	aft	aft	aft	aft	aft	aft	aft	aft	aft	aft	aft	aft	aft	aft	aft	aft	aft
															L Z	E W			L		L Y							
	Workmen's Train	Workmen's Train / Except Mons						Saturdays only.	Saturdays only. / One class only.		Workmen's Train / Except Sats.	Workmen's Train	Saturdays and School Holidays excepted.			Departs Caerphilly at 5 16 aft. see page 82.		15th July to 2nd Sept. / Except Sats.		Fris. only.				Saturdays only.	Saturdays only.	Except Saturdays. / Workmen's Train	Except Saturdays / One class only	Except Saturdays. Workmen's Train
Brecon ¶..........dep.			..	..	..	745	..	..	..	12 5				2 0			450		..	..		610	..	..			..	
Talyllyn Junction arr.			..	..	..	754	..	..	..	1214				2 9	..		459		..	..	..	619	..	..				
Talyllyn Junction dep.			..	..	..	756	..	..	..	1218				216	..		5 8		..	..	..	621	..	..				
Talybont-on-Usk........			..	..	..	8 1	..	..	..	1223				221	..		514		..	..	530	627	..	..				
Pentir Rhiw...........			..	..	..	815	..	..	..	1237				235	..		527		..	..	..	640	..	..				
Torpantau.............			..	..	..	830	..	..	..	1251				250	..		541		..	..	..	655	..	..				
Dolygaer ....(96			..	..	..	835	..	..	..	1258				254	..		546		..	..	..	659	..	..				
Pontsticill Junction arr.			..	..	..	839	..	..	..	1 2				258	450		550		..	..	6 6	7 3	..					
Merthyr N 96.. arr.			..	..	..	9 9	..		..	1 30				237	519		619		..		629	734	..					
Merthyr N 96.. dep.			..	..	..	810	..			12A10				238	525				4N0		633	..	..					
Pontsticill Junction dep.	..	..	..	..	..	844	..			1 5	..	..		3 1			Stp		528			7 7	..					
Pant 91...........arr.	..	..	..	..	..	847	..			1 9	..	..		3 4	Stp		..		531		Stp	711	..					
Dowlais (Central) 91 arr	..	..	..	..	..	9 2	..			1 29	..	..		315	..		..		..		..	722	..					
Dowlais (Central) 91 dep	..	..	..	..	..	835	..			1255	..	..		243	..		..		..		..	655	..		922		922	
Pant..............dep.	..	..	..	..	..	848	..			1 12	..	..		3 5	..		..		532		..	712	..		933		940	
Dowlais Top...........	..	..	..	..	..	853	..	1240		1 17	..	..		310	..		..	525	537		..	717	..		938		950	
Fochriw ¶.............	..	..	..	..	815	9 1	..	1248		1 26	..	..		318	..		..	532	544		..	724	853		945		959	
Darran and Deri.......	..	..	..	..	824	9 9	..	1257		1 35	..	..		326	..		..	541	553		..	733	9 1		954		109	
Bargoed 88............	..	..	..	..	829	917	..	1 5		1 42	..	..		335	..		..	548	6 0		aft	740	9 7		100		1015	
Pengam (Mon.) (above) arr	..	..	..	..	..	921	..	..		1 46	..	..		339	aft		aft	..	..		..	744	..	..	105		..	
Mls New Tredegar..dep.	6 2	620	725	830	..	..	11 0	..	1 25	..	142	238		..	355		5 3	..	..	610	710	..	..	925	..	950	..	1039
1½ Cwmsyflog..........	6 8	626	728	833	..	..	11 3	..	1 28	..	148	243		..	358		5 5	..	..	613	713	..	..	928	..	954	..	1044
2¼ Aberbargoed [(above)	614	631	733	838	..	..	11 8	..	1 33	..	154	248		..	4 3		510	..	..	618	718	..	..	933	..	101	..	1049
4 Pengam (Mon.) arr.	620	637	737	842	..	..	1112	..	1 37	..	159	254		..	4 7		513	..	..	622	722	..	..	937	..	107		1054
Pengam (Mon.)......dep.	..	638	738	843	..	922	1113	..	1 38	1 47	2 0	255		340	4 8		514	..	..	..	723	745	..	938	106	..		1055
Fleur-de-lis Platform...	..	641	741	846	..	926	1116	..	1 42	1 50	2 5	258		343	411		517	..	..	..	726	748	..	941	109	..		1058
Maesycwmmer B.........	..	644	747	850	..	930	1120	..	1 46	1 55	2 8	3 2		347	415		521	..	..		729	752	..	945	1012			11 2
Bedwas................	..		758	..	..	940	1130	..	1 55	2 5	220	312		356	425		531	..	..	..	..	8 2	..	955	..	..		1112
Trethomas.............	..		8 1	..	..	943	1133	..		2 8		315		359	428		534	..	..	..	..	8 5	..	958	..	..		1115
Machen 82.............	..		8 7	..	..	949	1139	..		2 13		320		4 4	436	524	539	..	..	..	..	810	..	103	..	..		1120
Church Road...........	..		812	..	..	954	1144	..		2 18		..		Aa	441	529	543	..	..	..	..	815	..	108	..	..		..
Rhiwderin.............	..		817	..	..	959	1149	..		2 23		..		413	446	534	548	..	..	..	..	820		1013	..	..		..
Bassaleg A....[125, 699	..		822	..	..	102	1152	..		2 27		..	4 0	417	450	538	552	..	..	..	..	824		1017	..	..	..	..
Newport 64, 69, 80, arr	..		830	..	..	109	12 1	..		2 35		..	410	427	458	546	6 1	..	..	..	..	832		1025	..	..	..	..

A About ¼ mile to Bassaleg Junction Station   A 1st and 3rd class   Aa Stops when required
B About ½ mile to Hengoed Sta   E Except Sats   H Thro Carrs. (one class only) commencing 29th July, Treherbert (dep 11 12 mrn) to Aberystwyth via Builth Wells, pages 84 and 150   K Thro Train to Llandrindod Wells (arr 3 14 aft) via Builth Wells, pages 84 and 150   L Sats only. 15th July to 2nd Sept   N or N One class only   S or S Sats. only
W Workmen's Train   Y Thro Train (one class only) Llandrindod Wells, (dep 4 15 aft) to Barry, via Builth Wells, pages 150 and 84   Y Arr 5 19 aft on Sats., 15th July to 2nd Sept

August 1939

June 1962

BRECON, MERTHYR, DOWLAIS and NEWPORT

WEEK DAYS ONLY

Miles		am W	am W	am	am	am	am	am	am	am	am	pm ②	pm W	pm	pm W	pm	pm W	pm	pm W	pm	pm	pm	pm	pm	pm	pm	pm	pm S	pm	pm	pm	pm W	pm W	pm W
			Except Saturdays	TC to Penarth (Table 125)		Except Saturdays and during School Holidays	To Hereford (Table 185)		To Builth Wells (Table 185)		To Hereford (Table 185)	Saturdays only	Except Saturdays	Saturdays only / TC to Cardiff (Queen Street)	Except Saturdays		Except Saturdays	To Moat Lane Junc. (Table 185)	Except Saturdays			Except Saturdays / To Hereford (Table 185)	To Moat Lane Junc. (Table 185)		Except Saturdays / To Three Cocks Junction (Table 185)	Saturdays only / To Hereford (Table 185)	Saturdays only		Saturdays only and commences 12th May 1962	Saturdays only Will not apply after 5th May 1962	Saturdays only / To Builth Wells (Table 185)	Except Saturdays	Except Saturdays	Except Saturdays
	Brecon .. .. dep	..	..	..	..	..	6 50	7 35	8 15	..	1025	..	..	..	..	1210	..	1 20	..	2 5	..	4 10	5 5	..	6 0	6 0	..	6 15	8 30	..	9 35	..	..	..
2	Groesffordd Halt	..	..	..	..	..	..	7 40	8 20	..	1030	..	..	..	..	1215	..	1 25	..	2 10	..	4 15	5 10	..	6 4	..	..	6 20	..	..	9 41	..	..	..
4	Talyllyn Junction arr	..	..	..	..	..	6 59	7 45	8 25	..	1035	..	..	..	..	1220	..	1 30	..	2 15	..	4 20	5 15	..	6 9	6 8	..	6 25	8 39	..	9 46	..	..	..
	Talyllyn Junction dep	..	..	..	..	..	..	7 46		..		..	..	..	..	1230	..		..	2 20	..	..		..	..	..	..	6 28	8 45	..	..	..	..	..
6¾	Talybont-on-Usk	..	..	..	..	..		7 52		..		..	..	..	..	1236	..		..	2 26	..	..		..	..	..	..	6 34	8 51	..	..	..	..	..
10	Pentir Rhiw	..	..	..	..	..		8 5		..		..	..	..	..	1249	..		..	2 38	..			..			..	6 50	9 3	..		..		..
14	Torpantau	..	..	..	..	..		8 20		..		..	..	..	..	1 5	..		..	2 53	..			..			..	7 6	9 17	..		..		..
15½	Dolygaer	..	..	..	..	..		8 24		..		..	..	..	..	1 10	..		..	2 58	..			..			..	7 10	9 22	..		..		..
17¼	Pontsticill Junction .. .. arr	..	..	..	..	..		8 28		..		..	..	..	..	1 14	..		..	3 2	..			..			..	7 14	9 26	..		..		..
24	120 Merthyr ② arr	..	..		..			..		..		..	..			..	..			..	..			..			..	7 47	..	..		..		..
	120 Merthyr ② dep	..	..		..			..		..		..	..			..	..			..	..			..			..	..	..	..		..		..
—	Pontsticill Junction .... dep	..	..		..		..	8 30		..		..	..			1 15	..			3 3	..			..			..	7 17	9 28	..		..	..	..
18¾	Pant .. .. arr	..	..		..		..	8 34		..		..	..			1 20	..			3 7	..			..			..	7 20	9 32	..		..	..	..
	Pant dep	5 13			..		..	8 35	..	..	..	..	..		1 10	1 22	..	..		3 8	..			..				7 21	9 33	9 33			9 34	
20½	Dowlais Top	5 20			..		..	8 40	..	..	..			1245	1 17	1 29		..		3 13	..			5 30				7 27	9 38	9 38			9 43	
21¼	Pantywaun Halt	5 27			..		..	8 43	..	..	..			1249	1 24	1 33		..		3 17	..			5 33				7 30	9 41	9 41			9 50	
23½	Fochriw	5 33		6 35	..		..	8 47	..	..	..			1254	1 29	1 38		..	2 25	3 21	..			5 38				7 35	9 45	9 45			9 55	
25½	Ogilvie Village Halt	5 42		6 42	..		..	8 52	..	..	..			1 1	..	1 43		..	2 33	3 27	..			5 43				7 40	9 51	9 51			10 4	
26	Darran and Deri	5 45		6 45	..		..	8 55	..	..	..			1 4	1 40	1 47		..	2 37	3 31	..			5 46				7 44	9 54	9 54			10 8	
28¼	Bargoed	5 57		6D58	..		..	9 0	..	..	..			1 10	1 46	1 56		..	2 46	3 36	..			5 52				7 51	10 0	10 0			1014	
45¼	131 Cardiff (Queen St.) .. arr	7 9	..	7 43	..		..	9 47	..	..	..	..	..	1 52	3 28	3§28	..	..	3 58	5 6	..	..	..	6 49		..	..	8 49	1049	1049	..	..	..	..
—	Mls New Tredegar .... dep	..	6 9	..	7 20	8 20	..	..	..	1052	..	1 0	1 30		..	..	2 41	..	..	..	4 5	..	..	..		..	7 10	..	..	..	..	9 40	..	1039
—	1¼ Cwmsyfiog	..	6 15	..	7 25	8 25	..	..	..	1058	..	1 6	1 35		..	..	2 47	..	..	..	4 9	..	..	..		..	7 15	..	..	..	..	9 45	..	1045
—	2¼ Aberbargoed	..	6 22	..	7 32	8 32	..	..	..	11 5	..	1 13	1 43		..	..	2 54	..	..	..	4 15	..	..	..		..	7 22	..	..	..	..	9 53	..	1052
29¾	Pengam (Mon.) .. .. .. dep	..	6 30	..	7 40	8 39	..	9 10	..	1113	..	1 22	1 52		..	2 2	3 4	..	..	3 43	4 24	..	..	..	..	..	7 30	8 3	..	..	..	10 6	..	11 2
30½	Fleur-de-lis Platform	..	6 34	..	7 43	8 43	..	9 14	..	1116	..	1 25	..		..	2 5	3 7	..	..	3 46	4 27	..	..	..	..	..	7 34	8 6	..	..	..	1010	..	11 5
31¾	Maesycwmmer B	..	6 37	..	7 47	8 46	..	9 18	..	1119	..	1 29	..		..	2 9	3 11	..	..	3 50	4 31	..	..	..	..	..	7 38	8 10	..	..	..	1016	..	11 9
36¼	Bedwas	..	6 48	..	7 58	..	..	9 27	..	1129	..	1 38	..		..	2 18	3 21	..	..	3 59	4 41	..	..	..	..	..	7 48	8 20	..	..	..	1025	..	1119
37½	Trethomas	..	6 52	..	8 1	..	..	9 31	..	1133	..	1 41	..		..	2 21	3 25	..	..	4 2	4 44	..	..	..	..	..	7 51	8 23	..	..	..	..	..	1124
39¼	Machen	..	6 57	..	8 7	..	..	9 36	..	1138	..	1 46	..		..	2 26	3 30	..	..	4 7	4 52	..	..	..	..	..	7 56	8 28	..	..	..	..	..	1129
44	Bassaleg A	..	..	..	8 22	..	..	9 49	..	1149	..	..	..		..	2 40	..	..	..	4 19	5 6	..	..	..	..	..	..	8 42	..	..	..	..	..	..
47	Newport .... arr	..	..	..	8 30	..	..	10 4	..	1158	..	2 6	..	..	..	2 48	..	..	..	4 27	5 13	..	..	..	..	..	8 17	8 50	..	..	..	..	..	..

A About ¼ mile to Bassaleg Junction Station
B About ½ mile to Hengoed Station

D Arr 6 52 am
S Saturdays only

TC Through Carriages
W Workmen's Train

② Second class only
§ On Saturdays arr 3 5 pm

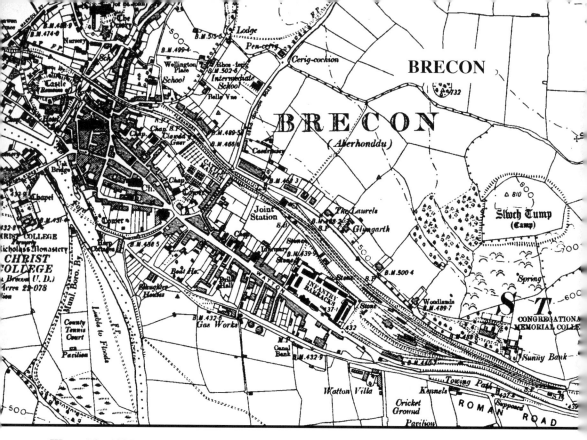

III.   The 1937 survey at 6 ins to 1 mile has the town centre on the left. Near the middle of this extract is "Joint Station", a term inapplicable since 1922. The Neath & Brecon Railway had reached Brecon from the west in 1867 and had its own terminus initially. The BMR's trains terminated at Watton (lower right), along with those from the east and north, until 1st March 1871. The Joint Station at Free Street took trains from the east and south from that date and from the north and west from 3rd August 1874.

1.   A long BMR train waits to depart for the south with 2-4-0T no. 25 of 1898 on the train and 0-6-0ST no. 28 of 1900 piloting. Originating from Robert Stephenson and Nasmyth Wilson, they were scrapped in 1922 and 1928 respectively. (R.K.Blencowe)

2.   Recorded on the turntable near the bay platform is Cambrian Railways' 4-4-0 no. 32, built by Robert Stephenson in 1897 and broken up in 1923. There was a staff of 46 here in that year. (LPC/P.Q.Treloar coll.)

IV. 1903 edition.

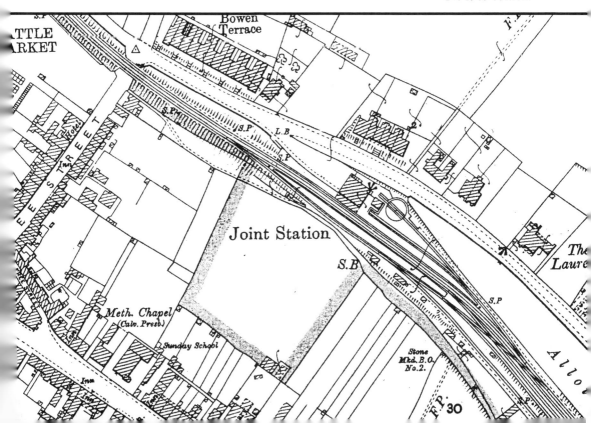

3. The station was built by the BMR and three other companies leased parts of it. Two of them took more than three years to agree terms, during which time some passengers had to walk between two of three stations. The west facade is seen in 1950. (LGRP/NRM)

4. A train destined for Hereford stands in the bay while the three through platforms are occupied. No. 12457 was one of a batch of 0-6-0s introduced by the Lancashire & Yorkshire Railway in 1889. (W.A.Camwell/SLS)

5.   No footbridge or subway was ever provided and so passengers used this unsupervised crossing at the west end. No. 3700 has just arrived from Newport on 4th August 1962 and is about to run round its train. The population then was just under 6000; a similar figure had applied 60 years earlier. (E.Wilmshurst)

6.   The final train was an SLS special on 2nd May 1964 which ran via Merthyr, from and back to Cardiff General. The two locomotives are running round and are seen from the signal on the right of the previous photograph. (Stations UK)

7.   Photographed a few minutes later, 2-6-2T no. 4555 was piloting 0-6-0PT no. 3690. The former survived to work on the Paignton & Dartmouth Railway, but the freshly ballasted track saw no more trains. (Stations UK)

8.   Later in 1964, the weeds were growing and the signal arms had gone. The 44-lever signal box had officially closed on 6th January 1963. The elegant and historic building was destroyed and a fire station appeared on the site. (Stations UK)

EAST OF BRECON

3462

9.   The locomotive sheds were established close to the Watton terminus and ex-MR no. 3462 is seen with part of the shed in 1922. The box controlling the signals was called "Brecon Junction". It was replaced by a ground frame in about 1931. (K.Nunn/LCGB)

V.   This map continues from the previous and includes the carriage shed which is not shown elsewhere. The ex-BMR engine shed is to the left of that of the Cambrian Railways.

10.   The station called "Watton" was named after the road leading to it and was retained for use as offices. A train passes on its way to Brecon on 6th July 1958. (R.M.Casserley)

11.   A westward view early in 1964 includes the cattle dock. Goods traffic ceased here on 4th May 1964, the ex-Neath & Brecon siding at Mount Street having closed on 31st December 1962. It was on the site of that railway's original terminus. (Stations UK)

12.　"On shed" in April 1954 were two ex-GWR 0-6-0PTs and two BR class 2 2-6-0s. The former types were generally used south and west, while the latter usually ran north and east. Diesels were never allocated here. (R.A.S.Marketing)

GROESFFORDD HALT

13.　　The platform was on the south side of the line and is seen after the last train had gone in 1964. The halt had opened on 8th September 1934. (Stations UK)

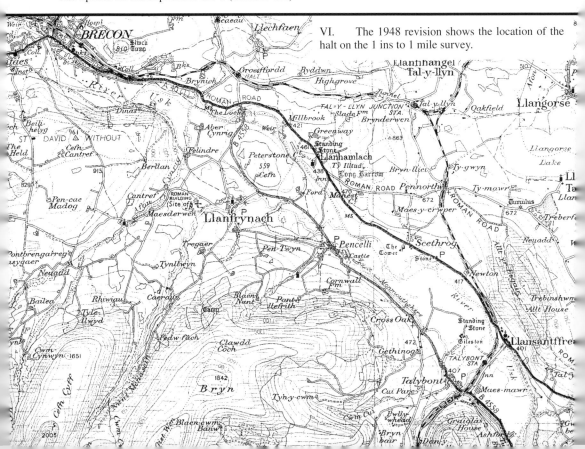

VI.　　The 1948 revision shows the location of the halt on the 1 ins to 1 mile survey.

TALYLLYN JUNCTION

VII.   The 1922 survey at 6 ins to 1 mile includes an engine shed built by the BMR in 1869, and in use until 1923. To the left of it is Brynderwen, which gave its name to a station which was in use until 1st October 1869. Only the north part of the loop is shown as double track. The LOOP LINE carried vast quantities of coal from South Wales, particularly during World War I. In the 1950s it saw seasonal trains between Pontypridd and Penychain, for Butlin's Pwllheli Holiday Camp.

14.   Two photographs from about 1939 show a train arriving from Brecon. Here it is emerging from the 674 yd long Talyllyn Tunnel. This had been opened for the tramroad on 7th May 1816. Although much enlarged for the railway, claims were made for it regarding it being the oldest in continuous use. The original gauge was about 3 ft 6 ins. (Stations UK)

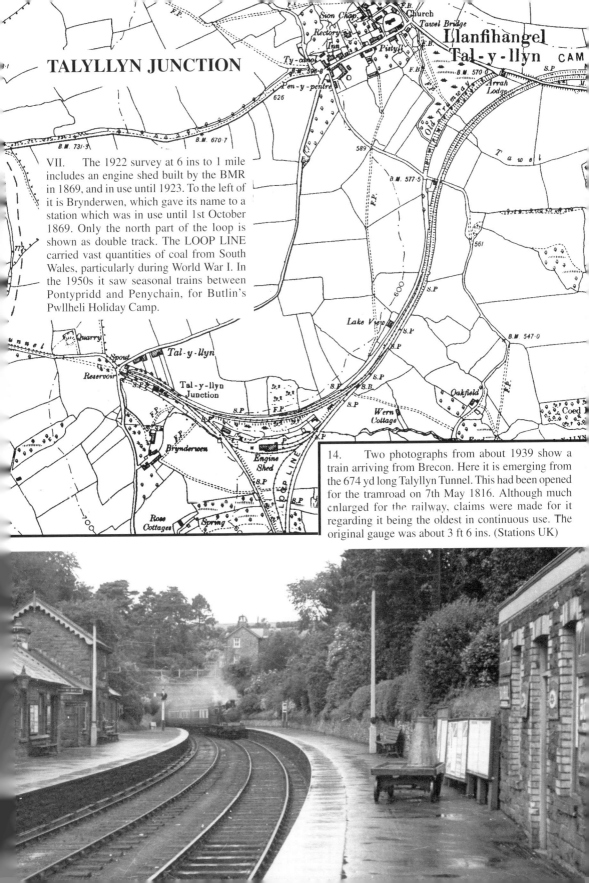

15.   Stepping back we see the same train close to West Junction Box and its associated glasshouse. The platform in the foreground was added in 1898 to allow two trains from Brecon to be present simultaneously. It was of particular value during times of late running. (Stations UK)

16.   No. 3638 waits to leave for Newport after another train has arrived at the opposite platform. Adjacent to this is the booking office, waiting room, refreshment room and toilets. These now form part of a private house. (D.Lawrence)

17.	No. 2236 runs in from Newport, while no. 46513 stands on the points, prior to departure to Three Cocks Junction. The signalman is on the foot crossing, which was also used by passengers. (Lens of Sutton)

18.   An eastward view in 1962 includes the cattle dock and the Pagoda shelter on the 1898 platform. The signal box dated from about 1887 and had 26 levers. The siding on the right served the public until 31st December 1962; those within the triangle were for exchange purposes. (P.J.Garland/R.S.Carpenter)

19.   The gloom of snow clouds descended on this unusual junction on the final day of operation. Ice had formed on the boards to add to the danger of crossing the lines here. (M.A.N.Johnston)

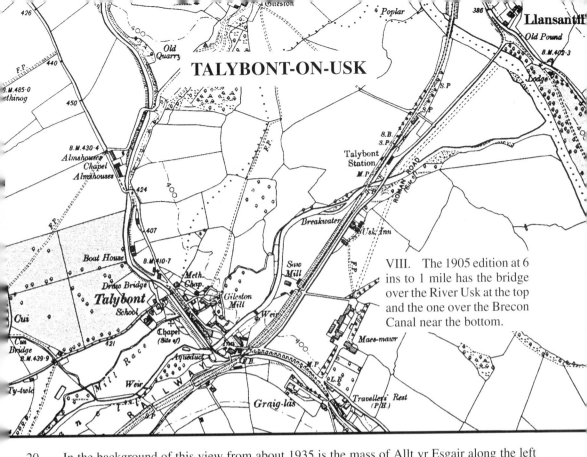

TALYBONT-ON-USK

VIII. The 1905 edition at 6 ins to 1 mile has the bridge over the River Usk at the top and the one over the Brecon Canal near the bottom.

20.   In the background of this view from about 1935 is the mass of Allt yr Esgair along the left foot of which ran the line before crossing the Usk. Double track extends into the distance, the line on the left running for more than a mile to Rock Siding, where the County Council used to unload roadstone. There were six men employed here in the 1930s. (Brunel University/Mowat coll.)

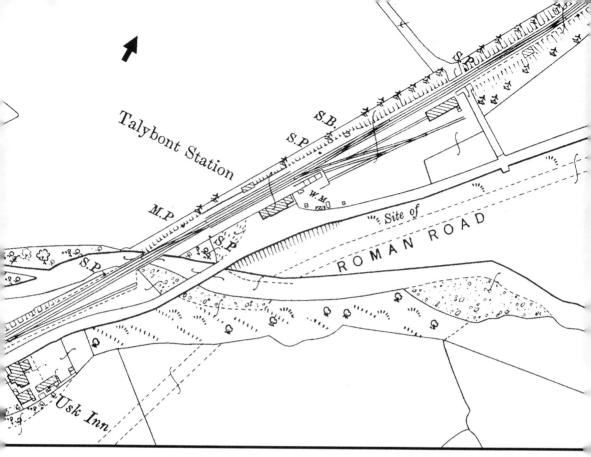

IX. A tributary of the River Usk runs across this 1903 survey.

21.   The exterior was recorded in August 1961, along with the goods crane, which was rated at six tons, and the engine shed. It was converted to a goods shed in about 1900. The 1200 gallon tank was supplied by a mile long pipe from the hillside. The building survives as an outdoor education centre. (Lens of Sutton coll.)

22.   A southward panorama shows the foot of "Seven Mile Bank", which was less famous than Shap and Lickey, but its 1 in 38 climb created equally exhilarating sound effects. The single siding was used by the engineers. One engine was limited to 12 full or 20 empty wagons. (LPC/NRM)

23.   Beyond the goods shed is the goods yard which remained open until 1st July 1963. In the distance is the former engine shed and the 17-lever signal box which was in use as late as 1st September 1963. (Stations UK)

Pant-y-rhiw

PENTIR RHIW

X.   The 1903 survey includes the farm which gave its name to the station and which was flooded for a reservoir. Officially opened in 1909, the platform is included in this survey.

F.P.

S.P

S.P

S.P

S.B

Pant-y-rhiw Station

BRECON &

24.   Having climbed continuously at 1 in 38 for three miles, a Pannier tank enters the short length of 1 in 60 in the loop. Drums of oil were required for the signal box and signal lights. (R.Holmes)

S.P

25. No. 3638 takes water at the north end of the loop, with the reservoir in the background. The runaway refuge siding runs to a point beyond the cottage shown in this and the previous picture. (D.Lawrence)

26. Although taken on a misty day in July 1958, this panorama is of interest as it includes the water tank and the siding signal to the left of it. The signal box opened on 11th January 1897 and had 20 levers. The platform served few people after the valley was flooded. (R.M.Casserley)

SOUTH OF PENTIR RHIW

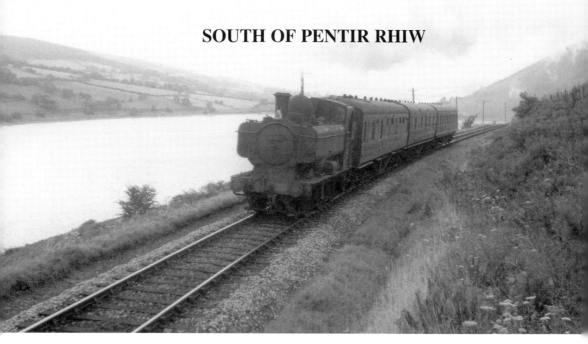

27.   Continuing one of the most breathtaking rail trips in Britain, our train climbs ever higher with the level surface of the lake emphasising the climb from the Usk Valley, by now in a hollow in the background. No. 3700 is approaching Torpantau Tunnel. (R.Holmes)

28.   Torpantau fixed distant signal and its 667yd long curved tunnel come into view near the summit of the climb. No. 46524 was working the 2.0pm from Brecon on 10th July 1958. (H.C.Casserley)

TORPANTAU

29. The station may not have opened with the line, but sidings for banking engines were provided here from the outset. The hillside drops away steeply beyond them into the Taf Fechan Valley in this 1956 southward view. (Brunel University/Mowat coll.)

XI. This map is a continuation of no. VI and reveals the circuitous course taken over the watershed of the Brecon Beacons. "Track of Old Rly." refers to the Bryn Oer Tramway, which connected with another that ran to the Rhymney Iron Works.

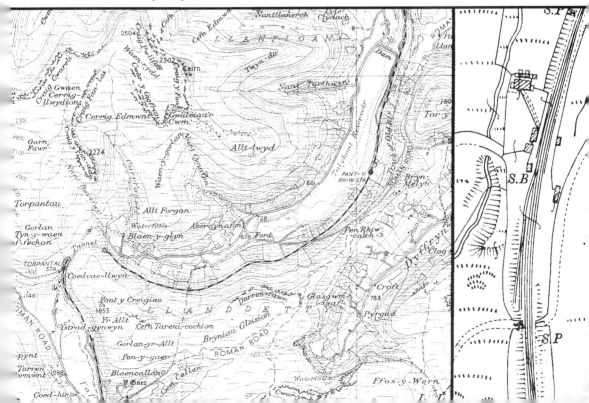

30.   Looking north from the 3.0pm from Newport on 12th July 1958, we can appreciate the magnitude of the ridge that separates South Wales from the rest of the Principality. The road passes over the tunnel and then climbs at 1 in 5. (H.C.Casserley)

31.   No. 3747 emerging from the tunnel, began the descent, which started at 1 in 138 through the station and then continued at 1 in 55. Note that the water tank is enclosed for protection against the severe weather. (R.Holmes)

32.   A photograph from August 1961 includes the single line tablet catcher and a notice nearby demanding a speed of 15mph. There was a staff of two recorded after 1931, presumably both signalmen operating the 13-lever frame. A stove was not provided initially! (Lens of Sutton coll.)

33.   A rare photograph from the goods-only era in 1963 includes a freight train from Brecon. The signal box and the line in the foreground were no longer used. Local goods had ceased on 1st June 1959 and the points by the box were removed soon afterwards. (Lens of Sutton coll.)

DOLYGAER

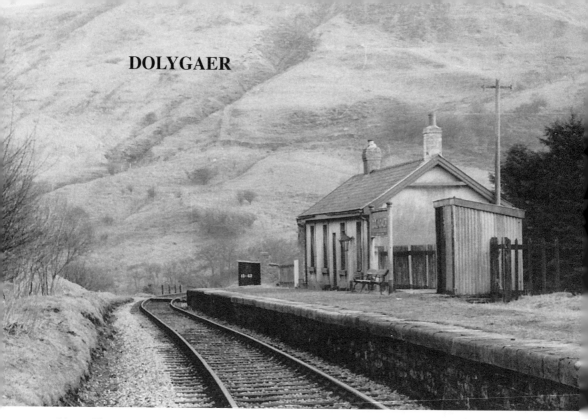

34.   There was one man employed here until staffing ceased on 21st March 1932. This view towards the south is from 1964 and shows the line descending at 1 in 47. (Stations UK)

XII.   The station is shown to be remote from habitation on the 1 ins to 1 mile map of 1948. The dashes and crosses represent the boundary between Glamorganshire and Monmouthshire and thus Wales and England. The Trevil Limestone Quarries and associated mineral railway are lower right. The reservoir northwards from the station is from 1862 and the part southwards was completed in 1927.

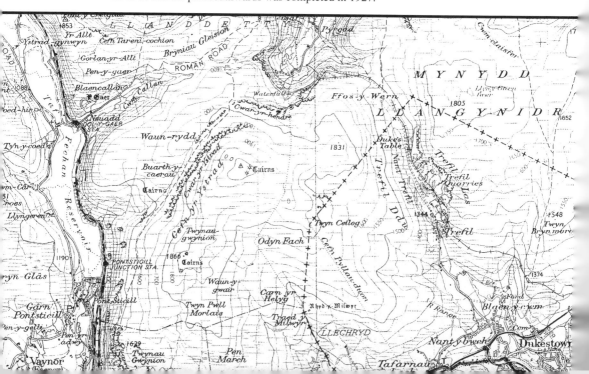

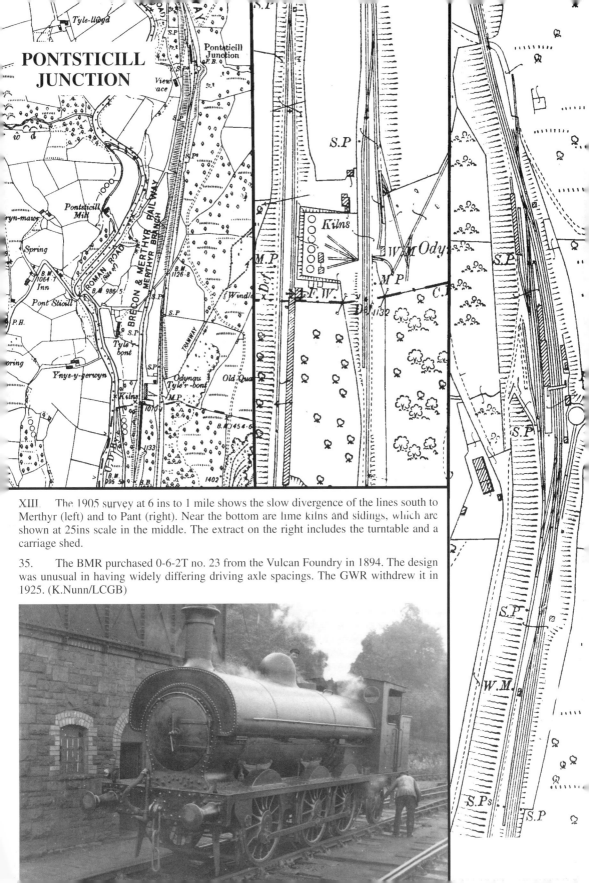

PONTSTICILL JUNCTION

XIII. The 1905 survey at 6 ins to 1 mile shows the slow divergence of the lines south to Merthyr (left) and to Pant (right). Near the bottom are lime kilns and sidings, which are shown at 25ins scale in the middle. The extract on the right includes the turntable and a carriage shed.

35. The BMR purchased 0-6-2T no. 23 from the Vulcan Foundry in 1894. The design was unusual in having widely differing driving axle spacings. The GWR withdrew it in 1925. (K.Nunn/LCGB)

36.   With the tranquil water of Taf Fechan Reservoir in the background, 0-6-0PT no. 7771 arrives from Brecon on 24th March 1937. No. 9647 waits on the left with the connection for Merthyr. The Brecon Beacons are still snow clad. (W.A.Camwell/SLS)

37.   No. 5793 was piloting no. 4635 on the through goods to Merthyr on 19th August 1950, when it was photographed outside the 52-lever signal box of 1885. Only the house remains standing today. (P.B.Whitehouse/Millbrook House)

38.   Seen from a train bound for Newport in July 1958 is the junction for Merthyr. The branch drops at 1 in 50 and continues at about that gradient for its entire six miles. Passenger service to Merthyr was withdrawn on 13th November 1961. (H.C.Casserley)

39.   A train of ammonia tanks waits in the distance alongside the goods yard which was in use until 31st December 1962. This photograph is from 1959 and includes the entrance to the station; it is by the handrail on the left. (R.E.Toop)

40.   No. 7736 obstructs the foot crossing as it takes water in the final months of passenger operation. Picture 35 was taken at this location. There was a staff of seven here back in 1923. (Stations UK)

41.   No. 2247 is heading a train for Newport on 17th September 1962, while 0-6-0PT no. 9776 stands with a train bound for Brecon. The signal box remained open until 4th May 1964, as freight traffic continued between Brecon, Merthyr and Dowlais Central until that time. (R.E.Toop)

BRECON MOUNTAIN RAILWAY

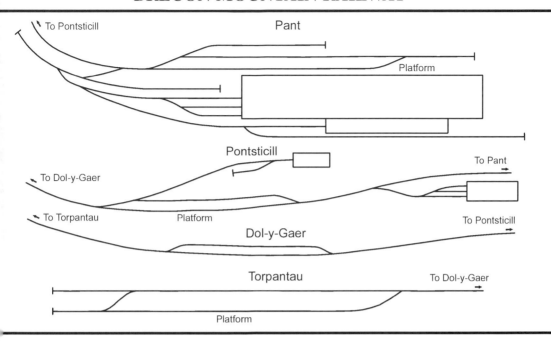

To Pontsticill

Pant

Platform

Pontsticill

To Dol-y-Gaer

To Pant

To Torpantau

Platform

To Pontsticill

Dol-y-Gaer

Torpantau

To Dol-y-Gaer

Platform

XIV. This leisure railway was laid to the gauge of 1 ft 11¾ ins, largely on the trackbed of the BMR from Pontsticill to Pant, and was opened on 8th June 1980. The track diagrams show the layout in 2003, although there was no opening date available for the Torpantau section. Trains had terminated at Dol-y-Gaer since 1994. The scheme included extension through Torpantau Tunnel eventually.

42. This photograph is from a similar angle as no. 36, but was taken on 30th June 1981 as Jung 0-6-2WT no. 1261 of 1908 was about to return to Pant. It is named *Graf Schwerin-Löwitz*. (T.Heavyside)

43.   South of the station is a carriage storage shed, which was built partially on the slightly lower ground once occupied by sidings alongside the line to Pant. The picture is from October 1998. (V.Mitchell)

44.   The locomotive seen in picture 42 is approaching Pant on 17th June 1994 on the length of fresh alignment. It has just used the final part of the BMR route, visible on the left. The switchback track in the foreground gives access to the works. The blocks were intended to retard a German invasion. (T.Heavyside)

45.	Spacious new premises were built; alongside is one of the LNWR's smoke ventilation shafts on Morlais Tunnel. The main entrance is seen from the car park in 1998. (V.Mitchell)

46.	Generous and thoughtful provision is made for visitors, both in the building and the coaches, the bodies of which have been built on wagon frames from South Africa. The Jung 0-6-2WT is seen in 1989. (T.Heavyside)

47. The workshops are well equipped to modern standards and in August 1997 contained a 1930 Baldwin 4-6-2. This had been wrecked in an accident at the Port Elizabeth Cement Works in 1973. The incident is illustrated in picture 4.10 in *Two-Foot Gauge Survivors* (Middleton Press). Vale of Rheidol engines are seen here sometimes, as the Brecon Mountain Railway took over that line in 1989. (P.G.Barnes)

48. After a prolonged restoration, the Baldwin was recorded leaving Pant in August 2002, the brake van being at the end of the platform. (Brecon Mountain Railway)

PANT

XV.   The junction is top left on this 1922 map at 6 ins to 1 mile. The BMR main line snakes across the page, with the LNWR roughly parallel and below it. This is featured in the companion album, *Abergavenny to Merthyr*, and is in Morlais Tunnel as it passes under the northern part of the BMR Dowlais branch. The two routes are joined by a small radius curve at Pen-y-Wern. Left of centre in the lower part of the map is the BMR's Dowlais terminus, while to the right is the GW & Rhymney Joint Railway terminus at Cae Harris.

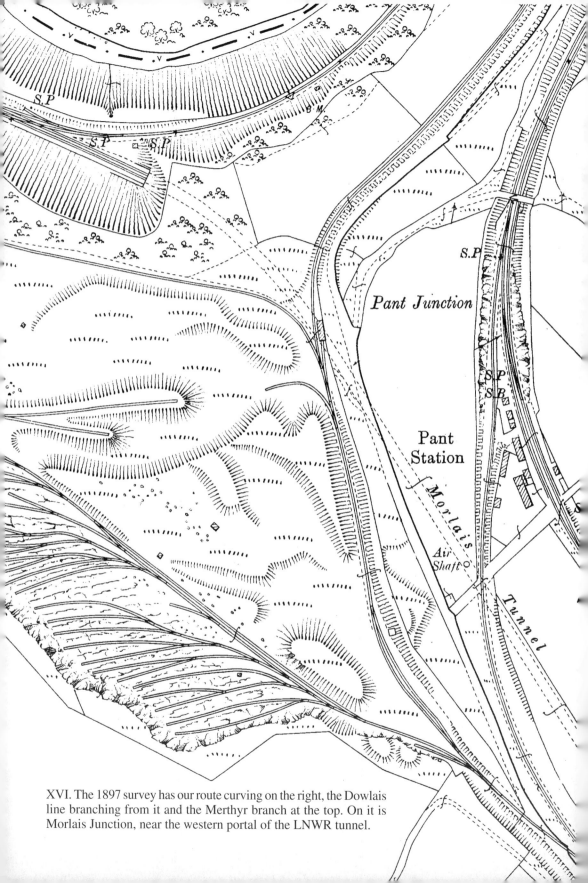

S.P

S.P   S.P

S.P

Pant Junction

S.P
S.B

Pant
Station

Morlais

Air
Shaft

Tunnel

XVI. The 1897 survey has our route curving on the right, the Dowlais
line branching from it and the Merthyr branch at the top. On it is
Morlais Junction, near the western portal of the LNWR tunnel.

49.   No. 18 was built by Sharp Stewart in 1881 and originally numbered 11. It ran until 1932 and is seen obstructing the foot crossing in 1922. There were four men employed here at that time. (K.Nunn/LCGB)

50.   The other photos of Pant date from about 1962 and take us northwards and then down the branch. Wide crossings were provided at both ends of the curved platforms. (Lens of Sutton coll.)

51.   The signal box was built in about 1881 and had 22 levers when closed on 31st December 1963. By that time, there was no room for any more huts.
(P.J.Garland/R.S.Carpenter)

52.   A southward view shows the branch to Dowlais Central dropping at 1 in 40 on the right. The refuge siding on the left has a catch point to protect the loop. There were no goods sidings. (M.Dart)

53. A train for Brecon stands on the left, while one for Dowlais Central is near the branch platform. On the right, smoke and steam issues from a ventilation shaft on Morlais Tunnel. The structure appears in picture 45. (SLS)

PANT and DOWLAIS													
Miles		**Week Days only**											
		a.m	a.m		a.m		p.m	p.m	p.m	p.m	p.m	p.m	p.m	p.m
		W	S					S	W	S	Ew		S	Ew
—	Pant............dep	7 28	8 50	..	9 55	..	1240	1 25	2 24	3 12	3 22	..	4 40	7 27	1115	11 22	..
¾	Pantysgallog Halt C...	7 31	8 53	..	9 58	..	1243	1 28	2 27	3 15	3 25	..	4 43	7 30	1118	11 25	..
1½	Dowlais (Central)...arr	7 34	8 56	..	10 1	..	1246	1 32	2 30	3 18	3 28	..	4 46	7 33	1121	11 30	..

(continued)

Miles		**Week Days only**										
		a.m	a.m		a.m		p.m	p.m	p.m	p.m	p.m	p.m	p.m
		W	S						Ew	S		S	Ew
—	Dowlais (Central)...dep	5 2	8 25	..	9 33	..	1220	1253	1 0	2 45	..	4 10	7 5	9 22	..	9 20	..
¾	Pantysgallog Halt C...	5 5	8 28	..	9 36	..	1223	1258	1 5	2 48	..	4 13	7 8	9 25	..	9 26	..
1½	Pant............arr	5 8	8 30	..	9 38	..	1225	1 0	1 7	2 51	..	4 15	7 10	9 27	..	9 28	..

C High Level
E Except Saturdays
S Saturdays only
W Workmen's Train

June 1951

June 1952

PANT and DOWLAIS													
Miles		**Week Days only**											
		a.m			p.m			p.m				p.m				
		W			Ew			Ew				Ew				
—	Pant............dep	7 28	..	..	2 24	..	..	3 27	..	..	..	11 22	..	..	..	
¾	Pantysgallog Halt D...	7 31	..	..	2 27	..	..	3 30	..	..	..	11 25	..	..	..	
1½	Dowlais (Central)...arr	7 34	..	..	2 30	..	..	3 35	..	..	..	11 30	..	..	..	
Miles		**Week Days only**											
		a.m			p.m			p.m								
		W			Ew			Ew								
—	Dowlais (Central)...dep	5 2	..	..	1 0	..	..	9 20	..	..	..	..	..	..	..	
¾	Pantysgallog Halt D...	5 5	..	..	1 5	..	..	9 26	..	..	..	..	..	..	..	
1½	Pant............arr	5 8	..	..	1 7	..	..	9 28	..	..	..	..	..	..	..	

D High Level
E Except Saturdays
S Saturdays only
W Workmen's Train

54. The branch trains did not often stop at the low level platform in later years, as they mostly reversed at Pant and passengers could use an upper platform during the run-round operation. (Lens of Sutton coll.)

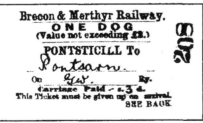

Brecon & Merthyr Railway.
ONE DOG
(Value not exceeding £2.)
PONTSTICILL To
Pontsarn
On GW. Ry.
Carriage Paid - s. 3 d.
This Ticket must be given up on arrival.
SEE BACK
205

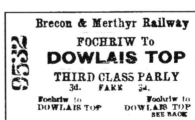

Brecon & Merthyr Railway
FOCHRIW To
DOWLAIS TOP
THIRD CLASS PARLY
3d. FARE 3d.
Fochriw to DOWLAIS TOP   Fochriw to DOWLAIS TOP
SEE BACK
9532   9532

Insurance   Ticket
FOR A SINGLE JOURNEY ON THE RAILWAY ON
In a Second Class Carriage from
DOWLAIS Stn. B&MRy
Sum assured £500 in case of death, or
£3 per week during total disablement, and
15s. per week during partial disablement
by injury. This ticket only covers injuries
caused by accident to the Train by which
the assured travels.
79

Gt Western Ry   Gt Western Ry
WORKMAN'S TICKET.
FOCHRIW   FOCHRIW
to
GROESFAEN COLLIERY PLATFORM
THIRD CLASS
3½d C   Fare   3½d C
FOR CONDITIO SEE BACK. (W.)
L393   L393

PANTYSCALLOG HALT

55.   This was the only intermediate stop on the Dowlais branch and it opened in June 1911. It is shown near the laundry at the centre of map XV. There was a station of the same name on the LNWR line. (Lens of Sutton coll.)

IVOR JUNCTION

56.   This was the point at which the LNWR joined the BMR's Dowlais branch. The connecting curve was not used by passenger trains. We witness an afternoon train from Dowlais to Pant approaching No. 2 Signal Box, the steps of which are on the right. Ivor Works Siding is on the left in this 1922 photograph of 0-6-0ST no. 18. The junction with the LNWR lines is at No. 1 Signal Box, behind the photographer. (K.Nunn/LCGB)

DOWLAIS CENTRAL

57.   No. 18 stands outside the engine shed in September 1922 on the occasion of its last trip in BMR ownership. It became GWR no. 1460. The station was given the suffix "Central" on 1st July 1924. (K.Nunn/LCGB)

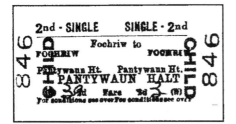

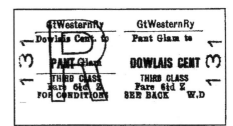

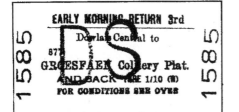

58.   Departing north on 30th November 1957 is 0-6-2T no. 5681. There had been a staff of 11 or 12 here in the 1930s and six private sidings to various industries. The goods shed (right) remained to become a youth centre and the site became a recreational area. (R.M.Casserley)

59.   This is one of the highest stations in Wales with a corresponding rainfall, but no shelter. Gas light would enhance the atmosphere at night. The dock line on the left served cattle pens. This and the following pictures are from 1962-63. (Stations UK)

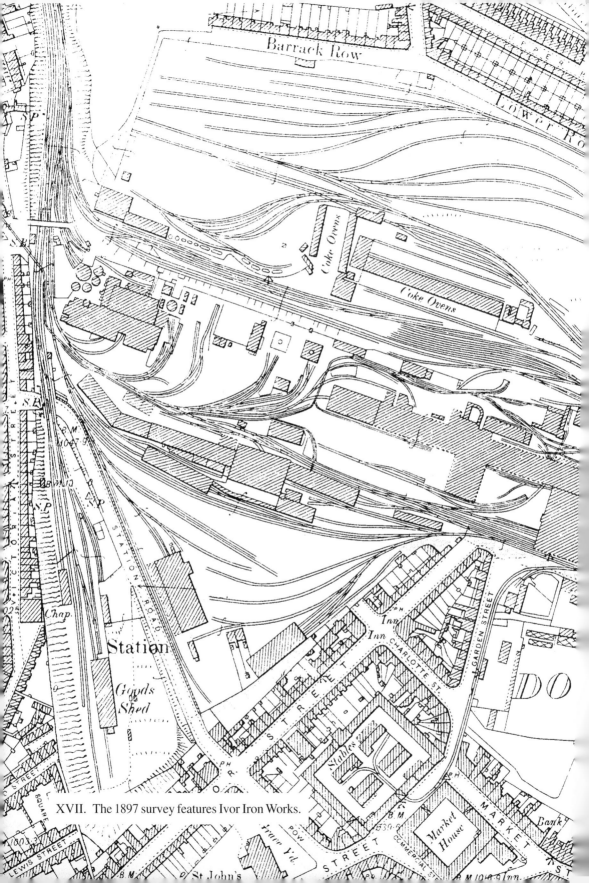

XVII. The 1897 survey features Ivor Iron Works.

60. The lofty position above the town is evident in this southward view, which features the disused engine shed. There was a population of 7453 in 1961, but back in the 1840s there had been over 12,000 men employed in the ironworks here. It was the last in the district and closed in 1987.
(R.S.Carpenter)

61. The wind battered engine shed is seen from the platform, which had last been used by regular passengers on 28th June 1952 and workmen on 2nd May 1960. The shed closed at that time.
(R.S.Carpenter)

62. The tall signal box is in the distance in this view of the yard which handled general goods traffic until 22nd November 1954, but continued with private siding consignments until 4th May 1964.
(Lens of Sutton coll.)

DOWLAIS TOP

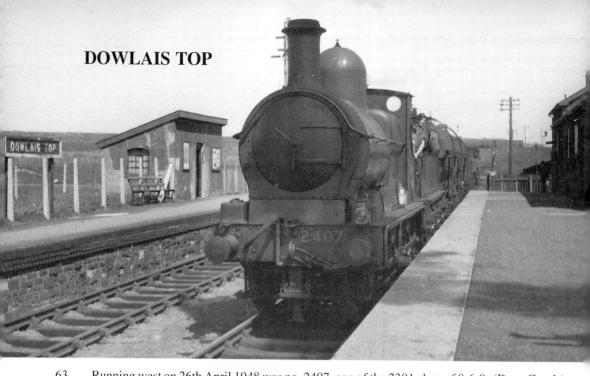

63.   Running west on 26th April 1948 was no. 2407, one of the 2301 class of 0-6-0s (Dean Goods) introduced in 1883 by the GWR. There were usually three men employed here between the Wars. (SLS)

XVIII. The 1897 edition shows the connection between the BMR single line and the double track of the LNWR. The former passes over the latter near the right border. The connection was eliminated in 1935, during the upgrading of the main road (A465 from 1919), which has a limestone railway crossing it on the level. The goods siding closed on 27th March 1961.

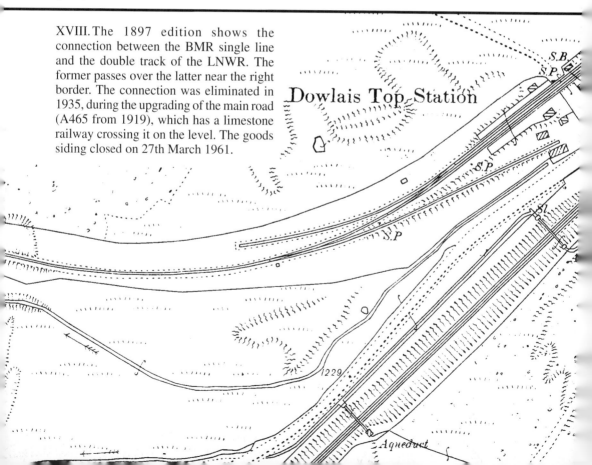

Dowlais Top Station

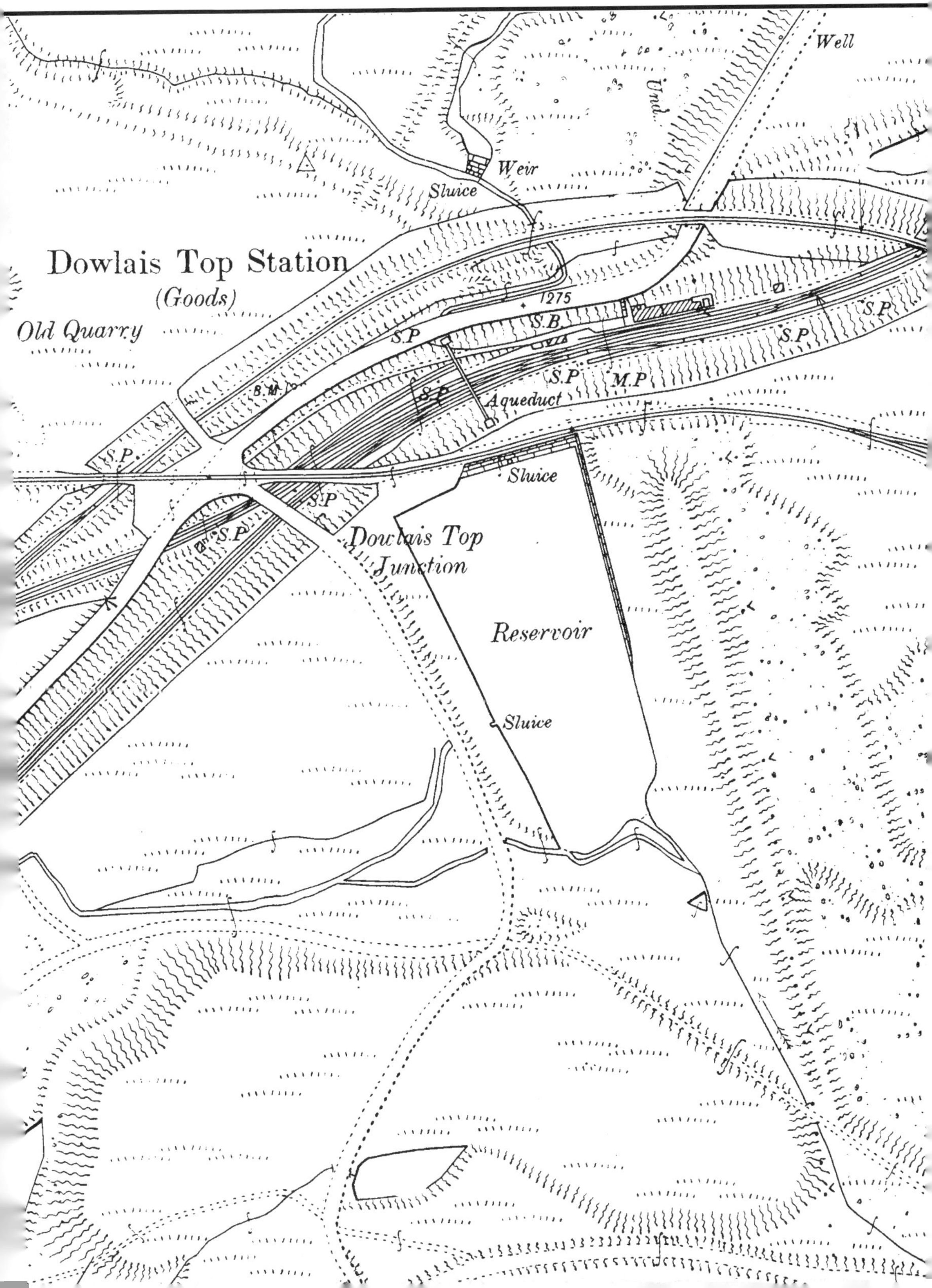

Well

Weir

Sluice

Dowlais Top Station
(Goods)

Old Quarry

1275

S.B.

B.M.

S.P.

S.P.

S.P.

S.P.

S.P.

S.P.

S.P.

M.P.

Aqueduct

S.P.

Sluice

S.P.

S.P.

Dowlais Top
Junction

Reservoir

Sluice

Und.

64.   No. 4635 was recorded on 11th August 1962 on a rescue mission to assist a failed passenger train. The bridge abutments once carried the Rhymney Limestone Railway and the cutting above the loco cab took the connection to the line illustrated in *Abergavenny to Merthyr*. (L.W.Rowe)

65.   The then-peaceful A465 is in the treeless landscape of this bleak upland and is viewed from a train bound for Newport on 27th January 1962. A small shrub adorns the nominal station garden. (P.J.Garland/R.S.Carpenter)

66.   The signal box was from 1876 or earlier and had 19 levers when it closed on 3rd August 1963. Winter can be severe at over 1200 ft above sea level. No. 9616 approaches as the hardy witness the last day of passenger working. (M.A.N.Johnston)

PANTYWAUN HALT

67.   The halt was opened on 22nd December 1941 to serve the tiny community at this windswept upland location. The scarred landscape is evident in this 1956 view, as is the unsurfaced track that provided alternative access. (H.C.Casserley)

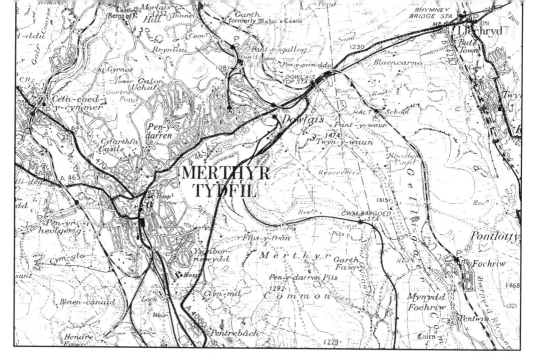

XIX.   The 1950 edition at 1 ins to 1 mile reveals the remote location of the halt and includes the ex-BMR branches from the top border to both Merthyr and Dowlais Central. Much of the area on the right has subsequently been subject to open cast working for coal.

FOCHRIW

68.   This southward view is from about 1910 and includes a glimpse of the goods yard, which remained open until the withdrawal of passenger services at the end of 1962. The staff level dropped from ten to five in the period 1923-35. (Lens of Sutton coll.)

XX. The previous map indicates that the colliery had connections to the lines in both adjacent valleys. This 1919 survey shows the proximity of the small dwellings to the station and the colliery.

Sewage Tank
(Disused)

S.P
S.P
S.B.
1144

MARTINS ROW

DYNEVOR STREET

RAILWAY TERRACE

GUEST STREET

Hall

School

Old Shaft

S.P

Station

Old
Coal Level

Brook Row

Capel

PLEASANT VIEW

MOORE'S ROW

291.9.423

AEL

P.O.

BRYN TEG TERRACE

GLYN TERRACE

PLANTATION TER.

Church

TRAMWAY

Shaft

Shaft

Fochriw Colliery

69.   The points to the goods yard are opposite the signal box which had 12 levers and was in use from March 1893 until August 1963. To the north, its companion at Fochriw Junction functioned between about 1911 and 1925. The background is devoid of trees, the station being 1150 ft above sea level. (LGRP/NRM)

70.   The staggering of the platforms becomes clear in this northward panorama from the 1950s. As was common on the BMR, passengers crossed the line on the level. (W.A.Camwell/SLS)

OGILVIE COLLIERY HALT

71.   The steps from the footbridge and the shelter are in place, but all signs have gone. The view is thus after 1962. The line north from Bargoed remained open for coal until 3rd September 1978, but was single from 8th November 1970. (Stations UK)

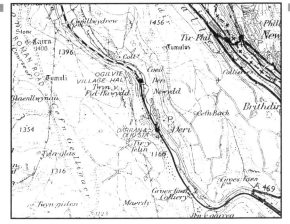

OGILVIE VILLAGE HALT

XXI.   The 1950 survey at 1 ins to 1 mile includes two collieries and two public stations. It also indicates the point at which double track commenced.

72.   The single platform came into use on 16th May 1935 and was staffed until 2nd May 1955. This northward view includes the line to Ogilvie Colliery. Access to it was controlled by Deri Junction box. (M.Hale)

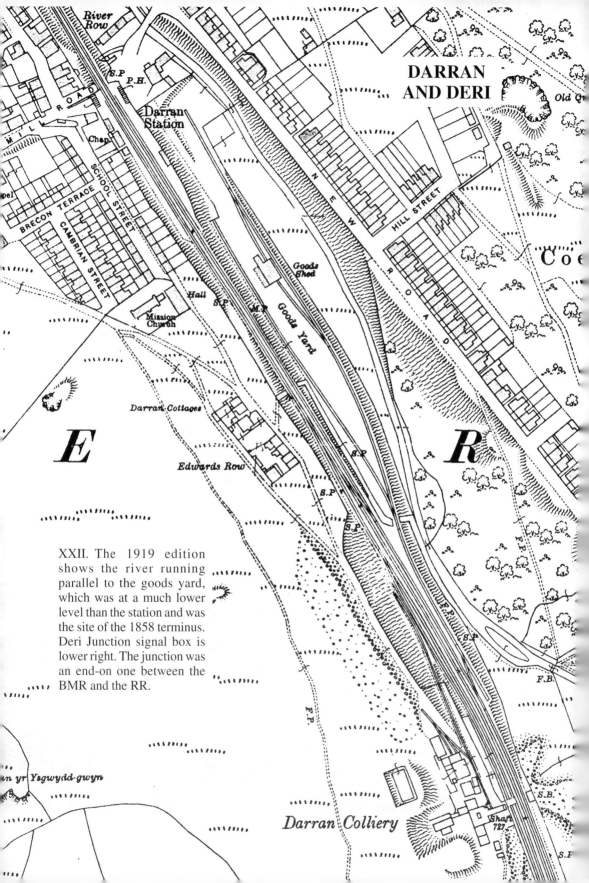

River Row

DARRAN AND DERI

ROAD

MILL

S.P.

P.H.

Darran Station

Chapel

Old Q

BRECON TERRACE

SCHOOL STREET

CAMBRIAN STREET

Coel

NEW

ROAD

HILL STREET

Goods Shed

Hall

Mission Church

S.P.

M.P.

Goods Yard

E

Darran Cottages

Edwards Row

S.P.

S.P.

S.P.

R

F.P.

F.P.

S.P.

XXII. The 1919 edition shows the river running parallel to the goods yard, which was at a much lower level than the station and was the site of the 1858 terminus. Deri Junction signal box is lower right. The junction was an end-on one between the BMR and the RR.

F.B.

F.P.

n yr Ysgwydd-gwyn

Darran Colliery

S.B.

Shaft 727

S.P.

73.   An Edwardian postcard view looking north reveals the steepness of the valley side, which is reflected in the next view. An inclined road passes under the line near the end of the platforms. (Lens of Sutton coll.)

74.   Trackwork was in progress near Mill Road to which steps descend from both platforms. The lower station was opened by the Rhymney Railway on 31st March 1858 and was a terminus until service was extended to Fochriw in 1865. This northward view is from the 1950s. (LGRP/NRM)

75. Looking south in July 1956, we have in the distance Groesfaen Colliery and Deri Junction signal box (20 levers) which was in use from about 1888 until 6th April 1964. Wagons stand on the approach to the goods yard, which was closed on 23rd August 1965. (H.C.Casserley)

GROESFAEN COLLIERY PLATFORM

76. The structure spanning the tracks is under cables carrying buckets of waste from the colliery to form one of the conical tips that once featured in the landscape of the area. The picture is from 11th June 1962. The platform was in use from about September 1926. (M.Hale)

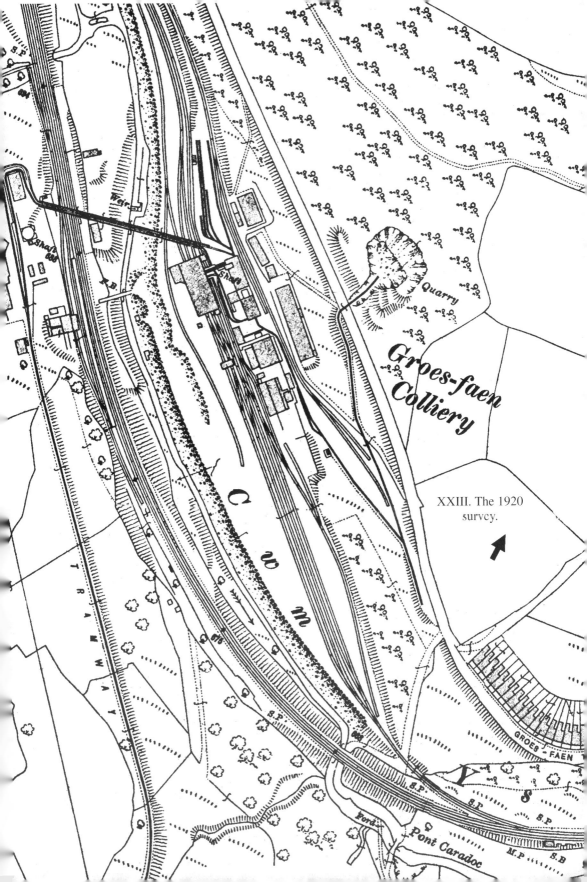

Groes-faen
Colliery

Quarry

Weir

Shaft

Cwm

TRAMWAY

GROES - FAEN

YS

SP

SP

SP

SP

MP

SB

Ford

Pont Caradoc

XXIII. The 1920
survey.

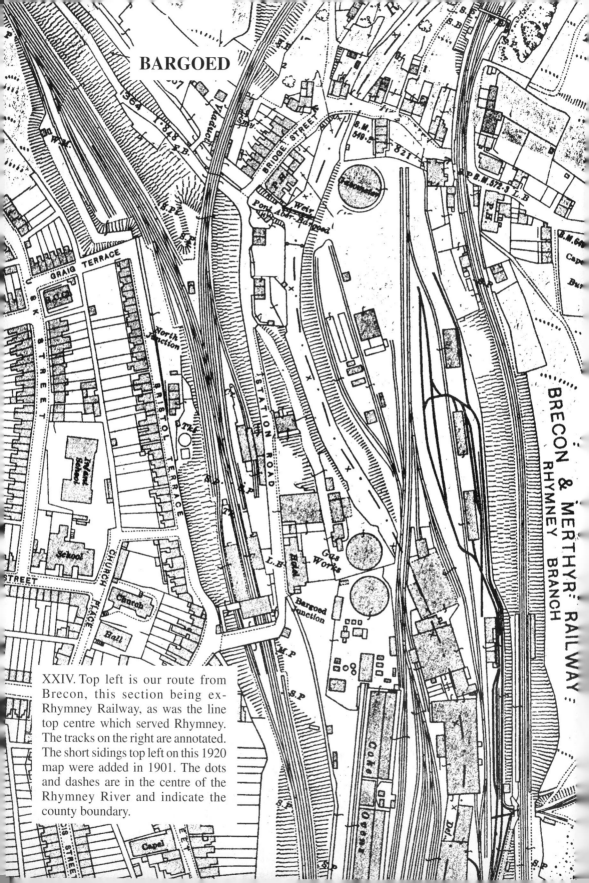

BARGOED

XXIV. Top left is our route from Brecon, this section being ex-Rhymney Railway, as was the line top centre which served Rhymney. The tracks on the right are annotated. The short sidings top left on this 1920 map were added in 1901. The dots and dashes are in the centre of the Rhymney River and indicate the county boundary.

BRECON & MERTHYR RAILWAY

RHYMNEY BRANCH

77.   A southward view in 1958 features the booking office, which was accessed from the side. The station was transferred to the GWR on 1st January 1922, along with other RR property. (Stations UK)

78.   A short goods train from the Brecon route passes the goods shed on 17th September 1962, hauled by 2251 class 0-6-0 no. 2218. Goods service at this station continued until 22nd March 1963. (R.E.Toop)

79.   A light snow covering greeted mourners on the last day of Brecon services, 28th December 1962. The signal box in the fork of the junction was termed "North" and closed on 9th November 1970 to be replaced by the one glimpsed in the next picture. The latter has 41 levers. (M.A.N.Johnston)

80.   Only the platform on the right of the previous picture was retained after 1970, but the line was signalled for bidirectional running. The other track was retained for northbound freight. The Rhymney branch is normally worked by DMUs, but on 18th March 2000 the 13.06 from Cardiff Queen Street was hauled by no. 47781, the platform on the right was restored in July 2001, by which time most services were operated by four-wheeled railbuses. A footbridge with lifts was provided. (D.H.Mitchell)

SOUTH OF BARGOED

81.   The three platform lines become two immediately south of the station. A class 2 2-6-0 departs for Newport and runs alongside a refuge siding as it approaches Bargoed South signal box, which closed on 28th January 1968. (D.Lawrence)

82.   From the same viewpoint about 20 years later we see the 13.28 Rhymney to Penarth DMU accelerating near Bargoed Colliery on 25th September 1980. All traces of mining were removed and the area was landscaped. (D.Mitchell)

NORTH OF PENGAM

(far left) XXV. Bargoed station is top left on this 6 ins scale map of 1922. South Junction is a little below it and at this point we leave the former Rhymney Railway, but run parallel to it, before crossing the valley to join the BMR line from Rhymney at Aberbargoed Junction. We then continue to Britannia Colliery, which is lower right.

83.   This is a northward postcard view of Britannia Colliery and includes trap points on the running line towards Bargoed. The sidings on the left were in use from about 1915 to 1958. Out of view on the left is Pengam Colliery North signal box. It had 27 levers when closed on 6th July 1964. (D.Edge coll.)

PENGAM (MON)

(left) XXVI.   The 1920 edition shows the goods yard to the left of the running lines. A new deep mine was completed in 1906, this increasing rail traffic greatly.

84.   The colliery complex is on the left as no. 3712 arrives from Newport in about 1950. There were 23 men employed here in 1923, but the figure had dropped to eight by 1934. (W.A.Camwell/SLS)

85.   A 1951 panorama includes the water tank and both water columns, together with the lamp room on the left. "Pengam" became "Pengam & Fleur-de-Lis" on 1st February 1909, "Fleur-de-Lis" on 1st July 1924 and "Pengam (Mon)" on 29th March 1926. There is now only one "Pengam" and that is on the Cardiff route. (LGRP/NRM)

86.   On the right in this 1958 view is the small goods yard which closed at the time of passenger service withdrawal, but one track remained to the colliery from the north until 1971. The line southwards was closed completely in 1967. Pengam Station signal box had 29 levers and was in use until 6th July 1964. (Stations UK)

87.   Looking north in April 1962 we see a 4200 class 2-8-0T at work in Britannia Colliery sidings and gain our only glimpse of the steps to the down platform. (H.B.Priestley/Milepost 92½)

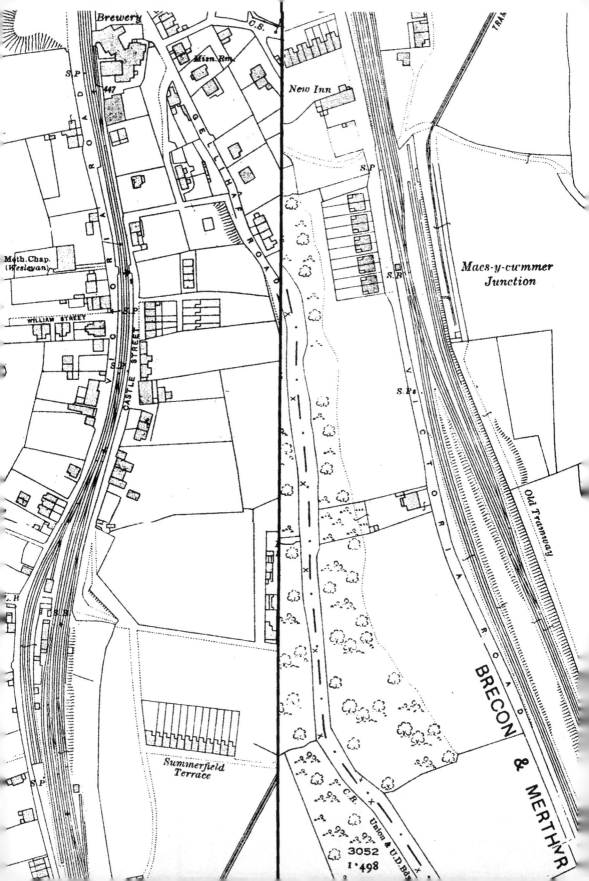

Brewery

O.S.

New Inn

Misn. Rm.

S.P

447

GELLIHAF

ROAD

S.P

Maes-y-cwmmer
Junction

S.B

Meth. Chap.
(Wesleyan)

WILLIAM STREET

S.P

CASTLE STREET

S.Ps.

S.B

VICTORIA

ROAD

Old Tramway

S.B

S.B

Summerfield
Terrace

BRECON & MERTHYR

S.P

C.B.

Union & U.D.Bdy.

3052

1·498

FLEUR-DE-LIS

←————————— XXVII. The platform was immediately to the north of the brewery siding, top left on this 1920 map. The stop opened on 29th March 1926 and this was the reason for the final name change at the previous station. Lower left are private sidings both sides of the running lines and also a signal box. This opened on 13th December 1892 as Carngethin Junction. It had 16 levers and became "Fleur-de-Lis North", closing in November 1928. The left map continues at the top of the right one, which includes the 29-lever Fleur-de-Lis South box. This also closed in 1928 and both were replaced by one with 55 levers mid-way between the two. It lasted until 18th August 1963. The tramway (top right) served Buttery Hatch Colliery. The track at the right margin curves east to the Sirhowy Valley, while we continue south for a further four miles. The former remained open to Tredegar Lower Junction until 4th September 1967, but the latter route closed completely to Bedwas at the end of 1962 although usable until August 1963.

88.   This shot is from a train bound for Brecon in July 1956. The name is reputed to have originated from an inn, although some say that it was brought by French immigrants. (H.C.Casserley)

89.   The southward view is from July 1959. The location was known locally as simply "The Flower". (H.C.Casserley)

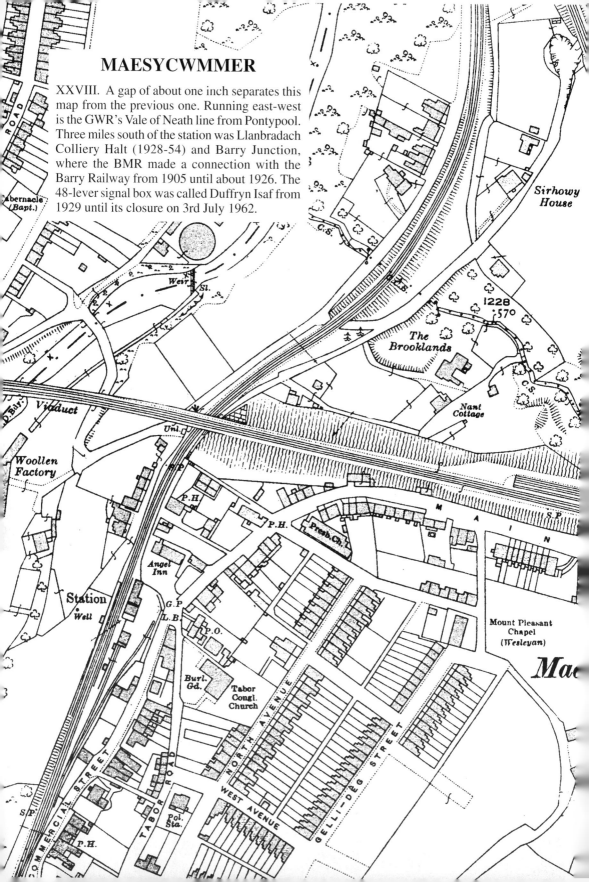

MAESYCWMMER

XXVIII. A gap of about one inch separates this map from the previous one. Running east-west is the GWR's Vale of Neath line from Pontypool. Three miles south of the station was Llanbradach Colliery Halt (1928-54) and Barry Junction, where the BMR made a connection with the Barry Railway from 1905 until about 1926. The 48-lever signal box was called Duffryn Isaf from 1929 until its closure on 3rd July 1962.

Sirhowy House

Abernacle (Bapt.)

Weir Sl.

1228
·570

The Brooklands

Nant Cottage

Viaduct

Unl.

Woollen Factory

P.H.

P.H.

Presb.Ch.

M A I N S.P.

Angel Inn

Station

Well

G.P

L.B

P.O.

Burl. Gd.

Tabor Congl. Church

Mount Pleasant Chapel (Wesleyan)

Mae

NORTH AVENUE

GELLI-DÊG STREET

WEST AVENUE

TABOR ROAD

COMMERCIAL STREET

Pol. Sta.

S.P.

P.H.

90.   An Edwardian postcard includes a section of raised platform, a feature often provided for the benefit of those handling milk churns. The crossover was moved north of the level crossing in 1927. (Lens of Sutton coll.)

91.   A 1956 photograph includes the 12-lever signal box which was operable until line closure. There was a staff of 15 in 1930, but only 10 in 1933. The lighting had been modernised to gas. (H.C.Casserley)

92.   This panorama was recorded from a train on the viaduct in July 1963. All services over it ceased on 16th June 1964. The suffix "& Hengoed" was applied between 1906 and 1924. All traffic ended on 30th December 1962. (P.J.Garland/R.S.Carpenter)

BEDWAS

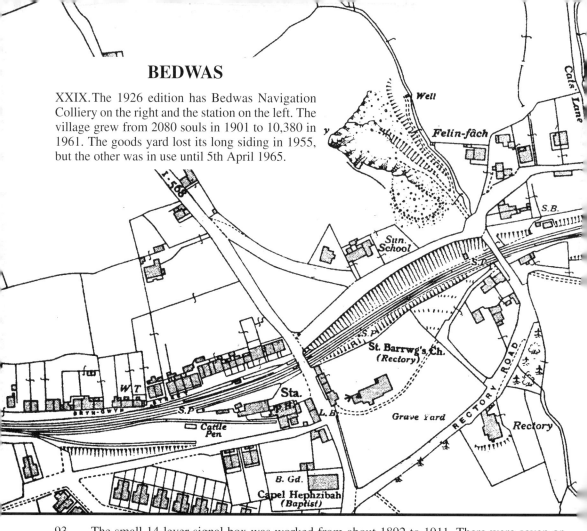

XXIX. The 1926 edition has Bedwas Navigation Colliery on the right and the station on the left. The village grew from 2080 souls in 1901 to 10,380 in 1961. The goods yard lost its long siding in 1955, but the other was in use until 5th April 1965.

93. The small 14-lever signal box was worked from about 1892 to 1911. There were seven or eight men here in the 1920s, but only four from 1932. (LGRP/NRM)

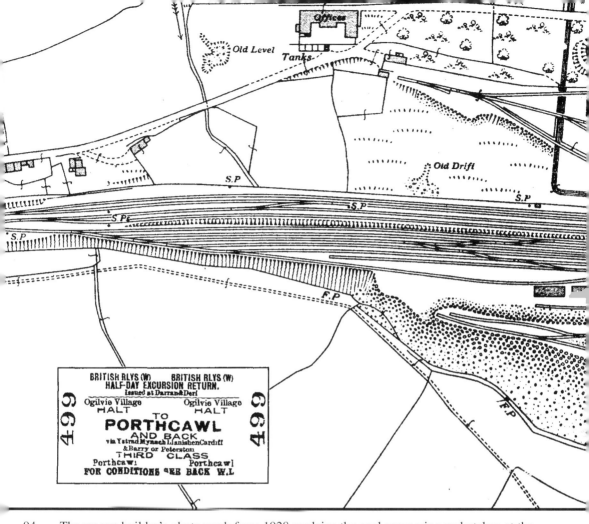

94.   The wagon builder's photograph from 1928 explains the coal processing undertaken at the colliery. Corner brackets were provided at one end only, as the other end opened. (Wakefield coll./R.S.Carpenter)

95.   The severe curvature presented a danger to those using the crossings seen in picture 93 and so these steps were provided from the down platform. The signal behind this Brecon-bound train in about 1950 is oddly positioned on account of the curve. (W.A.Camwell/SLS)

96.   The bridge parapet intrudes into this, the only view we have of the station frontage. The signal box was used for goods until replaced by this Pagoda shed. (Stations UK)

97.   Another photograph from 1962 and this features a somersault signal. It was worked from Bedwas Colliery North box, which is to the left of the join in the map. It had 40 levers and functioned until 17th December 1963. (H.B.Priestley./Milepost 92½)

98.   Although the line from Maesycwmmer Junction was closed completely in 1962, a connection to the colliery was retained from the east, albeit single line from 1965. This westward view is from February 1983; the colliery closed on 31st August 1985. (D.H.Mitchell)

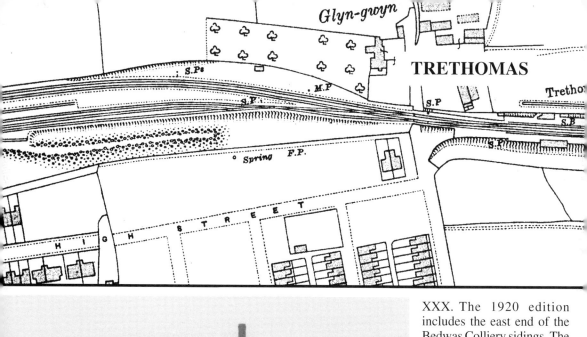

Glyn-gwyn

TRETHOMAS

Spring F.P.

HIGH STREET

XXX. The 1920 edition includes the east end of the Bedwas Colliery sidings. The station opened in about 1915 and spans the pages. There were public goods facilities from 1932 to 1964.

99. A 1952 panorama from the east includes the signals that gave access to the goods lines. There were up and down goods loops here. (LGRP/NRM)

100. The signal box opened in about 1911; its 50-lever frame was in use until 1964. There were about five employees here in the 1920s and eight from 1932. No. 3712 is westbound in the 1950s. (W.A.Camwell/SLS)

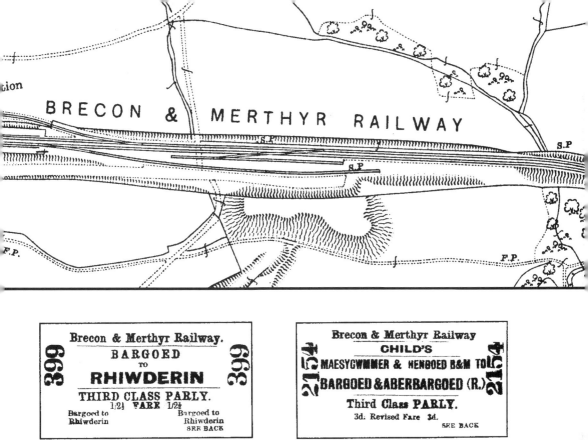

BRECON & MERTHYR RAILWAY

S.P.

S.P.

S.P.

F.P.

F.P.

Brecon & Merthyr Railway.

399

399

BARGOED
TO
RHIWDERIN

THIRD CLASS PARLY.
1/2½ FARE 1/2½

Bargoed to
Rhiwderin

Bargoed to
Rhiwderin
SEE BACK

Brecon & Merthyr Railway

2154

2154

CHILD'S

MAESYCWMMER & HENBOED B&M TO

BARGOED & ABERBARGOED (R.)

Third Class PARLY.

3d. Revised Fare 3d.

SEE BACK

101.   The Branch Line Society ran a special train on 19th February 1983 in non-photography weather. British Benzole & Coal Distillation Ltd ceased operating in November 1987, its complex stretching from Bedwas. (D.H.Mitchell)

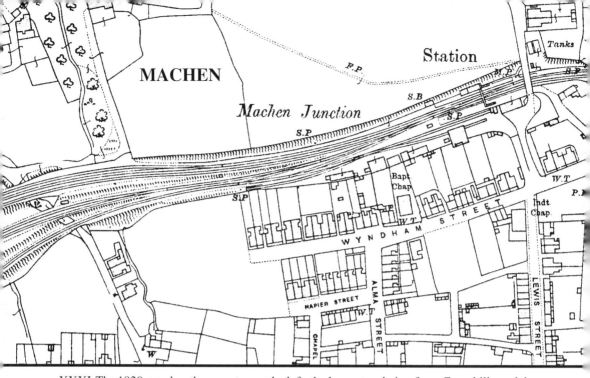

MACHEN

Machen Junction

Station

XXXI. The 1920 map has three routes on the left, the lower two being from Caerphilly and the upper one from Trethomas. The line at the top is a siding. The last of the three Caerphilly lines closed in 1967. On the right page is a short siding for P.D. Woodruff & Company's foundry, a down relief line, parallel lines for Vedw Colliery and, on the up side, tracks for Bovil Colliery.

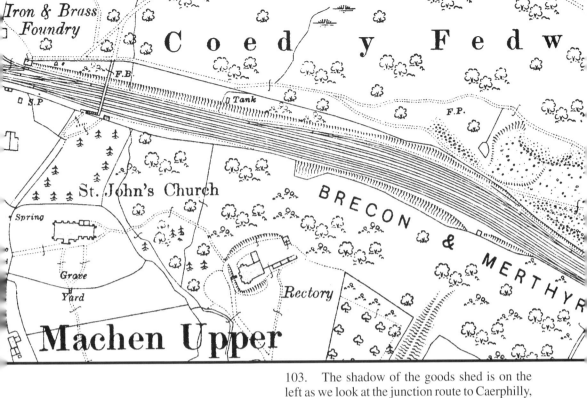

Iron & Brass
Foundry

Coed y Fedw

F.B

S.P

Tank

F.P

St. John's Church

Spring

BRECON & MERTHYR

Grave
Yard

Rectory

Machen Upper

102.   BMR 2-4-0T no. 9 is signalled for Bedwas. It was one of six built by R.Stephenson in 1904. There were 14 men at this station in 1923-24. (Lens of Sutton coll.)

103.   The shadow of the goods shed is on the left as we look at the junction route to Caerphilly, which branches left. It was opened for goods in 1864, passengers in 1887 and three intermediate halts were provided in 1904. Its history was most complex and involved four companies. (LGRP/NRM)

104. No. 351 was an ex-Taff Vale Railway 0-6-2T and is working autocoach no. 103 to Caerphilly on 13th September 1951. Workmen's trains continued on that route to and from Newport until 1st July 1963. (H.C.Casserley)

105. No. 2280 arrives with a train from Newport to Brecon sometime in the 1950s. The photograph was taken from the steps of Station signal box, which had 43 levers and continued in use until 20th November 1967, when the route to Caerphilly closed. The solitary wagon is a reminder that there was a goods yard here; it lasted until 16th July 1964. The building became a private house. (W.A.Camwell/SLS)

EAST OF MACHEN

106.   The BMR had its repair shops half a mile from the station, but the GWR closed them down on 19th March 1927. The Ministry of Supply found a new use for them from 1943 until about 1949, when they were photographed. Machen Shops signal box was at their west end until 15th July 1965. It had an 18-lever frame. Further east there were sidings for the limekilns of the Machen Stone & Lime Company. The sidings were still used by Hanson in 2003 and much railway ballast was loaded. (LGRP/NRM)

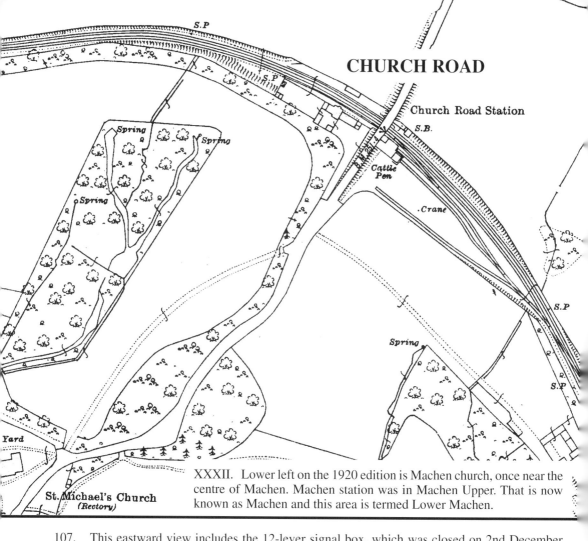

CHURCH ROAD

Church Road Station

S.B.

S.P

S.P

Cattle Pen

.Crane

Spring

Spring

Spring

Spring

S.P

S.P

Yard

St. Michael's Church
(Rectory)

XXXII. Lower left on the 1920 edition is Machen church, once near the centre of Machen. Machen station was in Machen Upper. That is now known as Machen and this area is termed Lower Machen.

107.   This eastward view includes the 12-lever signal box, which was closed on 2nd December 1963. It probably dated from the doubling of this part of the route in 1884. Staffing levels were five in 1923, but only two after 1933. There was no station staff after 1952 and trains ceased to call after 16th September 1957, goods included. The building became a private dwelling.
(Lens of Sutton coll.)

RHIWDERIN

108. This northward panorama has the station building lower left and a low bridge under the line to the right of it. This was supplemented by a level crossing with gates by 1900 and they gave way to simple lights on the road in June 1978. (Lens of Sutton coll.)

109. Beyond the station house is the goods yard, which closed on 14th September 1959. Passenger services ceased earlier, on 1st March 1954. This view predates that. (Lens of Sutton coll.)

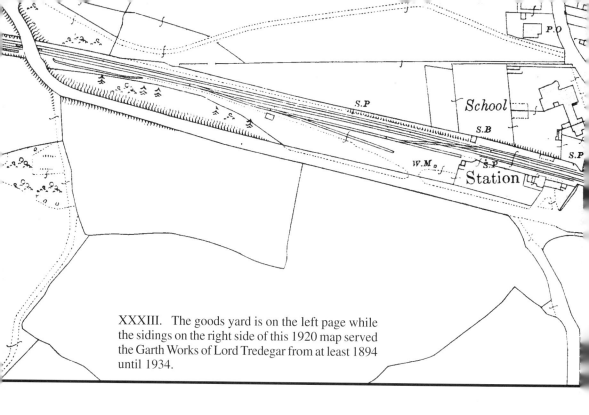

XXXIII. The goods yard is on the left page while the sidings on the right side of this 1920 map served the Garth Works of Lord Tredegar from at least 1894 until 1934.

110. The coping slabs have been removed prior to no. 4682 being photographed in the setting sun, running light engine. There had been four or five men here between the Wars. The building became a handsome residence. (Stations UK)

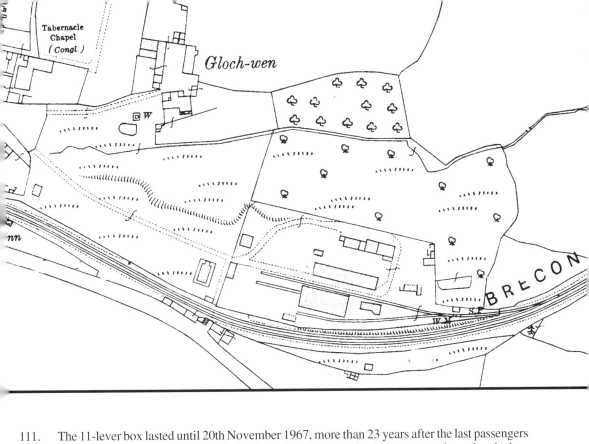

Tabernacle
Chapel
(Congl.)

Gloch-wen

W

nn

BRECON

111. The 11-lever box lasted until 20th November 1967, more than 23 years after the last passengers had left. It was acquired by the Caerphilly Railway Society and this close up was taken after the box had been moved to Caerphilly. It was eventually taken to the Teifi Valley Railway. (Stations UK)

RHIWDERIN

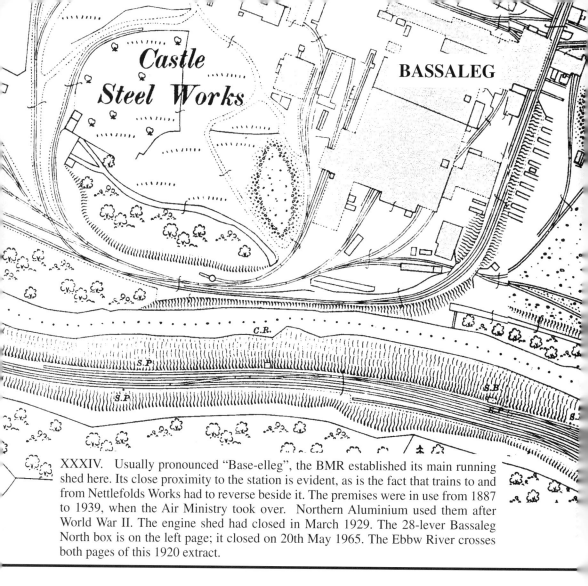

Castle Steel Works

BASSALEG

XXXIV. Usually pronounced "Base-elleg", the BMR established its main running shed here. Its close proximity to the station is evident, as is the fact that trains to and from Nettlefolds Works had to reverse beside it. The premises were in use from 1887 to 1939, when the Air Ministry took over. Northern Aluminium used them after World War II. The engine shed had closed in March 1929. The 28-lever Bassaleg North box is on the left page; it closed on 20th May 1965. The Ebbw River crosses both pages of this 1920 extract.

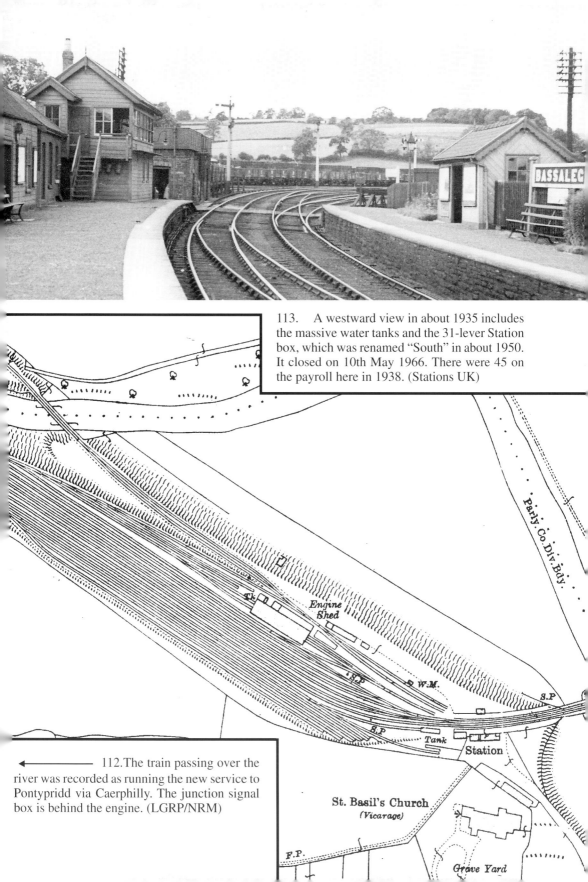

113.	A westward view in about 1935 includes the massive water tanks and the 31-lever Station box, which was renamed "South" in about 1950. It closed on 10th May 1966. There were 45 on the payroll here in 1938. (Stations UK)

←——— 112.The train passing over the river was recorded as running the new service to Pontypridd via Caerphilly. The junction signal box is behind the engine. (LGRP/NRM)

BASSALEC

Parly. Co. Div. Bay.

Engine Shed

S.P

S.W.M.

S.P.

S.P.

Tank

Station

St. Basil's Church
(Vicarage)

F.P.

Grave Yard

114.   This view across the Ebbw Valley is from the 1950s and includes the oddly positioned crossover which remained until 1965. The small goods yard (off the right of the picture) was open until 16th July 1964. The track on the right continued in use into the 21st century for stone trains. (W.A.Camwell/SLS)

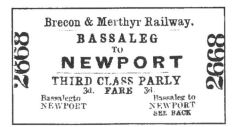

Brecon & Merthyr Railway.
BASSALEG
TO
NEWPORT
THIRD CLASS PARLY
3d.   FARE   3d.
Bassaleg to   Bassaleg to
NEWPORT   NEWPORT
                    SEE BACK
2668   2668

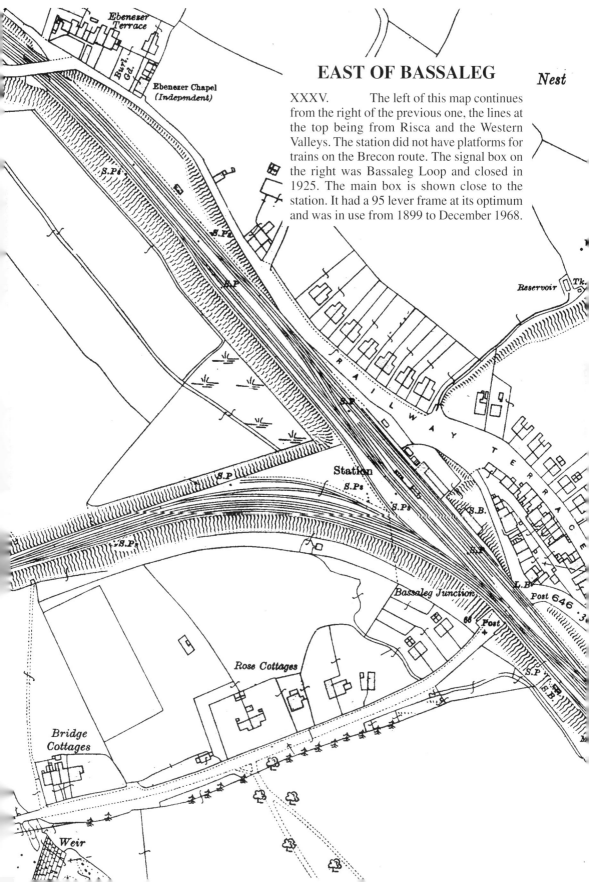

Nest

XXXV.   The left of this map continues from the right of the previous one, the lines at the top being from Risca and the Western Valleys. The station did not have platforms for trains on the Brecon route. The signal box on the right was Bassaleg Loop and closed in 1925. The main box is shown close to the station. It had a 95 lever frame at its optimum and was in use from 1899 to December 1968.

Ebenezer Terrace

Buri. Gd.

Ebenezer Chapel
(Independent)

S.P.

S.P.

S.P.

S.P.

S.P.

S.P.

S.Ps

S.Ps

Station

S.B.

S.P.

R A I L W A Y   T E R R A C E

Reservoir   Tk.

Bassaleg Junction

Post

L.B.

Post 646

Rose Cottages

Bridge
Cottages

Weir

S.P.

S.P.   S.B.

115.   A 1956 panorama from the south end of the island platform has the former BMR lines to the right of the nearest signals. On the far right are two further tracks which were in use from 1898 until 1963 and were known as the "Dock Lines". The route ahead was termed "Park Mile" and a toll was due to the landowner until 1923. There have been two single parallel freight lines from here to Park Junction since 1981. (Brunel University/Mowat coll.)

NEWPORT

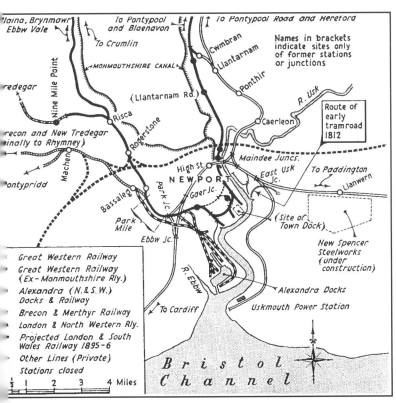

To Blaina, Brynmawr Ebbw Vale

To Crumlin

redegar

Nine Mile Point

MONMOUTHSHIRE CANAL

(Llantarnam Rd.)

recon and New Tredegar (inally to Rhymney)

Risca

Rogerstone

Machen

Pontypridd

Bassaleg

Park Mile

Park Jc.

Ebbw Jc.

To Cardiff

R. Ebbw

To Pontypool and Blaenavon

To Pontypool Road and Hereford

Cwmbran

Llantarnam

Ponthir

Caerleon

R. Usk

Names in brackets indicate sites only of former stations or junctions

Route of early tramroad 1812

Maindee Juncs.

High St.

NEWPORT

East Usk Jc.

To Paddington

Llanwern

Gaer Jc.

(Site of Town Dock)

New Spencer Steelworks (under construction)

Alexandra Docks

Uskmouth Power Station

Great Western Railway

Great Western Railway (Ex-Monmouthshire Rly.)

Alexandra (N.&S.W.) Docks & Railway

Brecon & Merthyr Railway

London & North Western Rly.

Projected London & South Wales Railway 1895-6

Other Lines (Private)

Stations closed

1 2 3 4 Miles

Bristol Channel

XXXVI. Before reaching our destination at High Street station our train will have passed over Park Junction, where the dock lines diverge, and Gaer Junction, where we join the main line. The tunnel north thereof was duplicated in 1912. (Railway Magazine 1960)

116. The first station had just two through platforms and a new station, as seen, was opened on 11th March 1880. The termini at Dock Street and Mill Street were then closed. The platform on the right was no. 1 and 2, no. 3 being a bay almost out of view. Trains up to London usually used nos 4 and 5. (Stations UK)

117.   No. 6 was adjacent to 4 and 5, no. 8 being on the left. This numbering was used from 1928 until 1961. These two photographs date from about 1935, this one including 0-4-2T no. 4831 with two autocoaches. (Stations UK)

118.   No. 8711 was recorded with the 3.0pm to Brecon at platform 3 on 12th July 1956. Only the front three coaches form the train. In 1938, there was a staff of 256 in the station, with a further 273 in the goods depot. (H.C.Casserley)

119.   Standing at the newly numbered platform 1 on 26th May 1962 is 0-6-0PT no. 9488 with a train for New Tredegar. This would run as far as Aberbargoed Junction before leaving the Brecon route. The DMU is destined for Birmingham New Street. (R.E.Toop)

120.   Our final look at a train for Brecon is shortly before service withdrawal, when cleaning of engines was a thing of the past on this route. The 0-6-0 is numbered 2247 under the grime. There had been nearly 100 years of service on this fascinating route for which there is much affection. (N W Sprinks)

Middleton Press

Easebourne Lane, Midhurst, W Sussex. GU29 9AZ Tel: 01730 813169 Fax: 01730 812601
Email: sales@middletonpress.co.uk   www.middletonpress.co.uk
If books are not available from your local transport stockist, order direct post free UK.

BRANCH LINES
Branch Line to Allhallows
Branch Line to Alton
Branch Lines around Ascot
Branch Line to Ashburton
Branch Lines around Bodmin
Branch Line to Bude
Branch Lines around Canterbury
Branch Lines around Chard & Yeovil
Branch Line to Cheddar
Branch Lines around Cromer
Branch Line to the Derwent Valley
Branch Lines to East Grinstead
Branch Lines of East London
Branch Lines to Effingham Junction
Branch Lines around Exmouth
Branch Lines to Falmouth, Helston & St. Ives
Branch Line to Fairford
Branch Lines to Felixstowe & Aldeburgh
Branch Lines around Gosport
Branch Line to Hayling
Branch Lines to Henley, Windsor & Marlow
Branch Line to Hawkhurst
Branch Line to Horsham
Branch Lines around Huntingdon
Branch Line to Ilfracombe
Branch Line to Kingsbridge
Branch Line to Kingswear
Branch Line to Lambourn
Branch Lines to Launceston & Princetown
Branch Lines to Longmoor
Branch Line to Looe
Branch Line to Lyme Regis
Branch Line to Lynton
Branch Lines around March
Branch Lines around Midhurst
Branch Line to Minehead
Branch Line to Moretonhampstead
Branch Lines to Newport (IOW)
Branch Lines to Newquay
Branch Lines around North Woolwich
Branch Line to Padstow
Branch Lines to Princes Risborough
Branch Lines to Seaton and Sidmouth
Branch Lines around Sheerness
Branch Line to Shrewsbury
Branch Line to Tenterden
Branch Lines around Tiverton
Branch Lines to Torrington
Branch Lines to Tunbridge Wells
Branch Line to Upwell
Branch Lines of West London
Branch Lines of West Wiltshire
Branch Lines around Weymouth
Branch Lines around Wimborne
Branch Lines around Wisbech

NARROW GAUGE
Austrian Narrow Gauge
Branch Line to Lynton
Branch Lines around Portmadoc 1923-46
Branch Lines around Porthmadog 1954-94
Branch Line to Southwold
Douglas to Port Erin
Douglas to Peel
Kent Narrow Gauge
Northern France Narrow Gauge
Romneyrail
Southern France Narrow Gauge
Sussex Narrow Gauge
Surrey Narrow Gauge
Swiss Narrow Gauge

Two-Foot Gauge Survivors
Vivarais Narrow Gauge

SOUTH COAST RAILWAYS
Ashford to Dover
Bournemouth to Weymouth
Brighton to Worthing
Dover to Ramsgate
Eastbourne to Hastings
Hastings to Ashford
Portsmouth to Southampton
Ryde to Ventnor
Southampton to Bournemouth

SOUTHERN MAIN LINES
Basingstoke to Salisbury
Crawley to Littlehampton
Dartford to Sittingbourne
East Croydon to Three Bridges
Epsom to Horsham
Exeter to Barnstaple
Exeter to Tavistock
London Bridge to East Croydon
Orpington to Tonbridge
Tonbridge to Hastings
Salisbury to Yeovil
Sittingbourne to Ramsgate
Swanley to Ashford
Tavistock to Plymouth
Three Bridges to Brighton
Victoria to Bromley South
Victoria to East Croydon
Waterloo to Windsor
Waterloo to Woking
Woking to Portsmouth
Woking to Southampton
Yeovil to Exeter

EASTERN MAIN LINES
Barking to Southend
Ely to Kings Lynn
Ely to Norwich
Fenchurch Street to Barking
Hitchin to Peterborough
Ilford to Shenfield
Ipswich to Saxmundham
Liverpool Street to Ilford
Saxmundham to Yarmouth
Tilbury Loop

WESTERN MAIN LINES
Bristol to Taunton
Didcot to Banbury
Didcot to Swindon
Ealing to Slough
Exeter to Newton Abbot
Newton Abbot to Plymouth
Newbury to Westbury
Oxford to Moreton-in-Marsh
Paddington to Ealing
Paddington to Princes Risborough
Plymouth to St. Austell
Princes Risborough to Banbury
Reading to Didcot
Slough to Newbury
St. Austell to Penzance
Swindon to Bristol
Taunton to Exeter
Westbury to Taunton

MIDLAND MAIN LINES
St. Albans to Bedford
Euston to Harrow & Wealdstone

Harrow to Watford
St. Pancras to St. Albans

COUNTRY RAILWAY ROUTES
Abergavenny to Merthyr
Andover to Southampton
Bath to Evercreech Junction
Bath Green Park to Bristol
Bournemouth to Evercreech Junction
Brecon to Newport
Burnham to Evercreech Junction
Cheltenham to Andover
Croydon to East Grinstead
Didcot to Winchester
East Kent Light Railway
Frome to Bristol
Guildford to Redhill
Reading to Basingstoke
Reading to Guildford
Redhill to Ashford
Salisbury to Westbury
Stratford upon Avon to Cheltenham
Strood to Paddock Wood
Taunton to Barnstaple
Wenford Bridge to Fowey
Westbury to Bath
Woking to Alton
Yeovil to Dorchester

GREAT RAILWAY ERAS
Ashford from Steam to Eurostar
Clapham Junction 50 years of change
Festiniog in the Fifties
Festiniog in the Sixties
Festiniog 50 years of enterprise
Isle of Wight Lines 50 years of change
Railways to Victory 1944-46
Return to Blaenau 1970-82
SECR Centenary album
Talyllyn 50 years of change
Wareham to Swanage 50 years of change
Yeovil 50 years of change

LONDON SUBURBAN RAILWAYS
Caterham and Tattenham Corner
Charing Cross to Dartford
Clapham Jn. to Beckenham Jn.
Crystal Palace (HL) & Catford Loop
East London Line
Finsbury Park to Alexandra Palace
Holborn Viaduct to Lewisham
Kingston and Hounslow Loops
Lewisham to Dartford
Liverpool Street to Chingford
London Bridge to Addiscombe
Mitcham Junction Lines
North London Line
South London Line
West Croydon to Epsom
West London Line
Willesden Junction to Richmond
Wimbledon to Beckenham
Wimbledon to Epsom

STEAMING THROUGH
Steaming through Cornwall
Steaming through the Isle of Wight
Steaming through Kent
Steaming through West Hants

TRAMWAY CLASSICS
Aldgate & Stepney Tramways
Barnet & Finchley Tramways

Bath Tramways
Brighton's Tramways
Bristol's Tramways
Burton & Ashby Tramways
Camberwell & W.Norwood Tramways
Clapham & Streatham Tramways
Croydon's Tramways
Dover's Tramways
East Ham & West Ham Tramways
Edgware and Willesden Tramways
Eltham & Woolwich Tramways
Embankment & Waterloo Tramways
Exeter & Taunton Tramways
Fulwell - Home to Trams, Trolleys and Buses
Great Yarmouth Tramways
Greenwich & Dartford Tramways
Hammersmith & Hounslow Tramways
Hampstead & Highgate Tramways
Hastings Tramways
Holborn & Finsbury Tramways
Ilford & Barking Tramways
Kingston & Wimbledon Tramways
Lewisham & Catford Tramways
Liverpool Tramways 1. Eastern Routes
Liverpool Tramways 2. Southern Routes
Liverpool Tramways 3. Northern Routes
Maidstone & Chatham Tramways
Margate to Ramsgate
North Kent Tramways
Norwich Tramways
Reading Tramways
Seaton & Eastbourne Tramways
Shepherds Bush & Uxbridge Tramways
Southend-on-sea Tramways
South London Line Tramways 1903-33
Southwark & Deptford Tramways
Stamford Hill Tramways
Twickenham & Kingston Tramways
Victoria & Lambeth Tramways
Waltham Cross & Edmonton Tramways
Walthamstow & Leyton Tramways
Wandsworth & Battersea Tramways

TROLLEYBUS CLASSICS
Bradford Trolleybuses
Croydon Trolleybuses
Derby Trolleybuses
Hastings Trolleybuses
Huddersfield Trolleybuses
Maidstone Trolleybuses
Portsmouth Trolleybuses
Reading Trolleybuses

WATERWAY ALBUMS
Kent and East Sussex Waterways
London to Portsmouth Waterway
West Sussex Waterways

MILITARY BOOKS
Battle over Portsmouth
Battle over Sussex 1940
Blitz over Sussex 1941-42
Bombers over Sussex 1943-45
Bognor at War
Military Defence of West Sussex
Military Signals from the South Coast
Secret Sussex Resistance
Surrey Home Guard

OTHER RAILWAY BOOKS
Index to all Middleton Press stations
Industrial Railways of the South-East
South Eastern & Chatham Railways
London Chatham & Dover Railway
London Termini - Past and Proposed
War on the Line (SR 1939-45)